Half-title page: *A cyclo driver awaits his fare on a busy Hanoi street.*
Frontispiece: *Cafes such as Mr Ly's, peopled in the past by foreign correspondents and local literati, are now patronised not only by tourists but by a burgeoning Vietnamese middle class as well.*
Pages 4 -5: *Enterprising young girls contribute to the family's kitty by selling newspapers to local businessmen travelling between Hanoi and Ho Chi Minh City on the Reunification Express.*
Page 6: *The resilience of their fathers brought peace, which these off-duty army cadets can now enjoy.*
Pages 8-9: *In his time, grandfather would be happy if he had two meals a day. Today, with excess produce, his grandson can look forward to more.*

PHOTO CREDITS

All photographs in this book are from **Photobank, Luca Invernizzi Tettoni** except for the following: pages 2, 19, 25 (centre), 27 (bottom), 31 (top), 33 (top inset), 36 (second from bottom), 39 (top), 41 (bottom inset), 44-45, 46, 47, 48 (bottom), 50 (top left and bottom), 54, 56-57 (main picture), 62 (bottom), 64 (top, left and right; bottom, centre and right), 65 (bottom), 67 (top right), 79 (bottom left), 82 (bottom left), 84, 92 (top right), 100 (bottom left), 101 (top), 106 (bottom), 121 (bottom left), **Image Bank**; 16 (top right, bottom), 17 (bottom), 30, 42 (top left and centre left), 43 (top left), 50 (centre left), 51 (top right), 55 (bottom left), 60, 63, 64 (centre, left and right), 65 (top left), 72, 73 (bottom), 76 (bottom), 77, 78, 79 (top right), 83 (right), 96 (top right), 97, 98-99, 100 (top, centre and bottom right), 111 (bottom left), 120, **Bes Stock**; 15, 36 (bottom), 37, 38, 39 (centre), 43 (centre and bottom left), 62 (top left), 76 (right inset), 79 (top left and centre left), 80-81, 85 (centre and bottom left), 88 (bottom left), 90, 91, 96 (top left), 110 (top right), 115 (top left), 116 (bottom right), 121 (centre), 124, 125 (top left and centre), 126 (centre), **Perly & Joe Photography**; 1, 31 (bottom right), 40-41 (main picture), 64 (top centre), 66, 67 (top left), 73 (centre), 74-75, 93 (bottom), 96 (centre), 116 (top left), 126 (top left), **HBL Network**; 52, 53 56 (top inset), **Morten Strange**; 14, 18, 55 (top right), 59 (top left, bottom left and right), 108-109, **Mark De Fraeye**; 33 (bottom inset), 36 (top left), 51 (top left), 55 (top left), 58, 89 (top left), 123 (inset), **Jill Gocher**; 8-9, 55 (centre), 73 (top), 76 (top left), 89 (centre), **David Simson**; 88 (top left, centre and bottom right),116 (bottom left), **Hutchinson Library**; 36 (centre top), 48 (top left), 56 (bottom inset), **Ingrid Horstmann**; 89 (bottom), **Mick Elmore**; 17 (top), **Hulton Getty Picture Collection Ltd**; 51 (bottom right), **Camera Press**; 59 (centre right), **Björn Klingwall**; 85 (top left), **Axiom Photographic Agency.**

Series Editor: K E Tan
Designer: Tuck Loong
Picture Researcher: Susan Jane A. Manuel
Production Manager: Anthoney Chua
Printed in Singapore

First published in 1997. Reprinted 2004

Published by Times Editions – Marshall Cavendish
An imprint of Marshall Cavendish International (Asia) Private Limited
A member of the Times Publishing Limited
Times Centre, 1 New Industrial Road, Singapore 536196. Tel: (65) 6213 9288 Fax: (65) 6285 4871
E-mail: te@sg.marshallcavendish.com Online Bookstore: http://www.timesone.com.sg/te

Malaysian Office:
Federal Publications Sdn Berhad (General & Reference Publishing) (3024-D)
Times Subang, Lot 46, Persiaran Teknologi Subang, Subang Hi-Tech Industrial Park, Batu Tiga,
40000 Shah Alam, Selangor Darul Ehsan, Malaysia.
Tel: (603) 5635 2191 Fax: (603) 5635 2706 E-mail: cchong@tpg.com.my

National Library Board (Singapore) Cataloguing in Publication Data
Lim, Kwee Lan.
Vietnam : land of the ascending dragon / text, Lim Kwee Lan ; photographs,
Photobank ... [et al.]. – Singapore : Times Editions, c1997.
p. cm.
ISBN : 981-204-777-8
1. Vietnam – Social life and customs. 2. Vietnam – Guidebooks. I. Title.
DS556.3

959.7 -- dc21   SLS97095557

VIETNAM
LAND OF THE ASCENDING DRAGON

VIETNAM
LAND OF THE ASCENDING DRAGON

Text
LIM KWEE LAN

Photographs
PHOTOBANK
LUCA INVERNIZZI TETTONI

and

IMAGE BANK, BES STOCK,
PERLY & JOE PHOTOGRAPHY, HBL NETWORK

TIMES EDITIONS

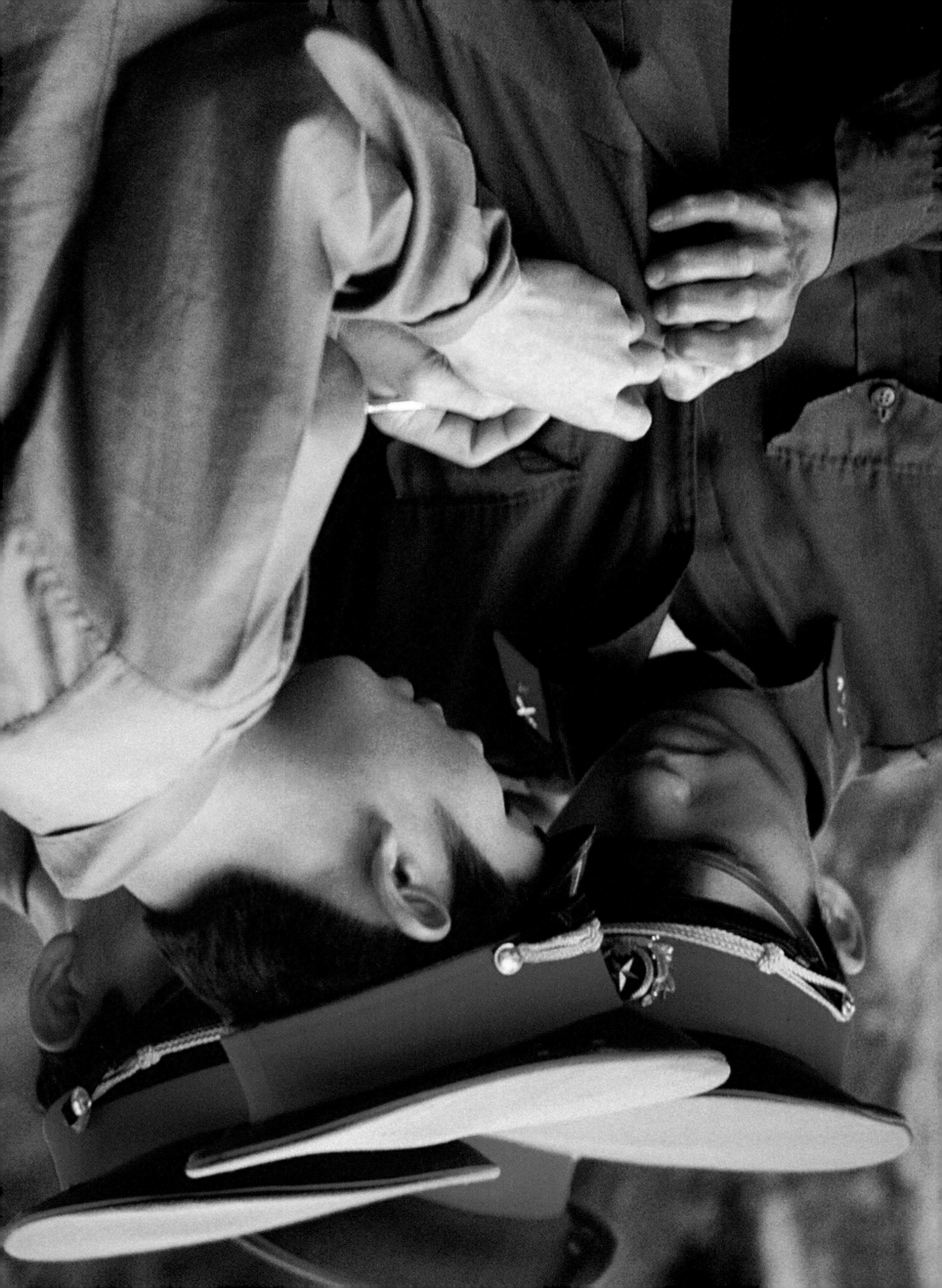

CONTENTS

INTRODUCTION

Vietnam enjoyed a brief reputation as a romantic outpost of the French but lost much of it after its closure from a succession of wars and its advocacy of communism. Its inaccessibility to the world became both a blessing and a curse. It affected the country so badly that just the mere mention of its name conjured up images of ruthless guerrillas and hardline communists, a perception made more disturbing by American war movies and the plight of the boat people, who risked their lives on the high seas to flee their country.

Since the reopening of its doors, perspectives of the country have changed tremendously. Vietnam is no longer a geographic and economic pariah, but is fast becoming a keen competitor to her East Asian neighbours. And, unlike them, it has not lost its charm to rapid industrialisation.

Its people still possess the grace of an ancient culture and its landscape is relatively untouched by the march of progress. Limited contact with the world has blessed this ancient civilisation with a unique blend of unspoiled cultural and physical beauty.

This natural beauty is everywhere. In the north, cloud-covered mountains reach for the heavens. Stretching across the east and centre, the highlands are covered by slopes of verdant rain forests, extending over a good three-quarters of the country. Here, the Montagnards, 54 distinct minority tribes with their own costumes, customs and languages live, preserving their traditional way of life. Down in the rich alluvial deltas of the south and the northwest, padi farmers in conical hats stoop to their backbreaking labour. In the west, the mountains meet the sea and brown-sailed junks skirt a spectacular coastline of white beaches and narrow sand dunes to glide on stunning lagoons. Indeed, it is difficult to remain unmoved amidst such diverse beauty, just as it is hard not to be captivated by its colourful history.

For the culture of ancient civilisations has always been enthralling to modern men. And Vietnam's long and rich past, which spans 4,000 years, provides enough fuel for the romantic. So ancient is this history that it is traced through myths and legends of dragons and kings, deities and heroes. Even the origin of the country is linked with a legend. So diverse is Vietnam's culture that religions such as Buddhism, Confucianism, Taoism, Christianity and Islam converge with animism and ancestor worship. All these religious strands are even fused into one in Cao Dai, a belief indigenous to the Vietnamese. And this rich culture comes alive in the religious festivals and rituals observed by its people, its architecture and its ancient art of water puppetry.

But central to the charm of Vietnam is its people. Despite suffering decades of hardship, they remain gentle and warm, even to their former enemies. Ask the lacquer-toothed grandmother for permission to take her photograph and she breaks into a ready smile. Corner a swanky office worker for street directions and he walks you to your destination. They touch the heart with their graciousness, making the beauty of Vietnam more complete and the romance and charm, more inevitable.

*Words do not capture adequately the beauty of Vietnam, evidenced in the graciousness of her people (left)
and the unspoilt splendour of her landscape (above and following pages).*

HISTORY AND THE VIETNAMESE

T he Vietnamese will tell you with pride that their cultural heritage is not confined to 2,000 years of recorded history. Another 2,000 may be shrouded in myths but they are kept alive in the memory of the people through songs, legends and religious rituals. One such legend, which explains their origins, also accounts for the Vietnamese conviction that they came from the same womb.

It is believed that the union between Lac Long, the Dragon Lord of the Mighty Seas, and Au Co, Princess of the High Mountains, yielded a hundred sons. Convinced that their differences prevented conjugal bliss, they parted. Only when their sons grew up, each governing a principality, did they reunite in the spirit world.

The most powerful of these principalities was Van Lang, which included present-day North Vietnam and the northern part of Central Vietnam. The kingdom, which thrived from 2879 to 258 B.C., had 18 successive kings and was known as the Hung Vuong Dynasty.

The legend remains a romantic myth, but archaeological studies suggest the presence of an ancient civilisation with the discovery of prehistoric bronze drums of the Dong Son culture, dating back to 500 B.C. These 2,000 years of legend gradually merged with another 2,000 of recorded history, beginning with the first period of Chinese occupation in 111 B.C.

When the Chinese conquered the Red River Delta, they found a feudal society based on fishing, hunting and slash-and-burn agriculture. During their thousand year rule, the Chinese introduced fine art, education and agricultural techniques to their vassal state. Despite this exposure to Chinese culture, the Vietnamese retained their strong national identity, even fighting for it in short-lived spells of independence through the Trung sisters and the scholar Ly Bon.

Chinese rule ended in A.D. 939, to be succeeded by a string of independent dynasties. The period was marked by the southward extension of the Vietnamese territory through the marriage of a Tran princess to the King of Champa and a brief period of Chinese occupation which saw the imposition of the conqueror's culture over the literature, art and history of the vanquished.

The strong Vietnamese will to independence, which the Americans were to encounter centuries later, reasserted itself and the longest of these self-ruling dynasties, the Le Dynasty (15th to 18th centuries), was formed. Not only did the Le emperors sack the Chinese, they also broke free from the cultural and intellectual domination of the Chinese civilisation, giving prominence to Vietnamese traditions in law, religion and literature. It was during this period that the southern kingdom of Champa was assimilated and the first volume of national history written.

So intricately involved in the history of Vietnam is Ho Chi Minh that everywhere, there are reminders of his contribution to the country's independence. From the personal altar (left) to the grand mausoleum where his body rests (above), Uncle Ho's image gazes benignly at his fellowmen.

Unfortunately, the later Le successors were inept and corrupt, resulting in the partition of the country under the rule of the Trinh lord in the north and the Nguyen lord in the south with the emperor existing in a purely ceremonial capacity. Frequent rebellions marked the final years of the two courts, culminating in the Tay Son uprising, led by three brothers.

One of the Tay Son brothers ruled as Emperor Quang Trung till the end of the 18th century when the successor of the Nguyen lord in the south, Nguyen Anh, gained control of the country through the help of a French missionary. In exchange for territorial and trading rights, the French armed Nguyen with modern military techniques. Having seized Hanoi, he proclaimed himself Emperor Gia Long.

For the first time in two centuries, the country was united and renamed Viet Nam. Thirteen Nguyen emperors ruled from the 18th to the 19th centuries from their new administrative capital in Hue. They left a legacy of Chinese-influenced architecture—mostly splendid pagodas, temples, palaces and mausoleums—with the exception of the penultimate Nguyen emperor, Khai Dinh, who built one blending oriental and occidental architecture. The extravagance of the Nguyen rulers is epitomised by the reign of Tu Duc, who had 50 chefs prepare an equal number of dishes served by as many servants at every meal. His tea was made of dew drops that had condensed overnight on lotus leaves.

But the Nguyens are not only remembered for their contribution to Hue architecture. They made serious efforts to develop a national administration patterned on Confucian philosophy. But most of all, the founder of the dynasty gave the French a foothold in Vietnam.

French traders and missionaries were already entrenched in the South when the emperor, wary of their growing influence, revoked trade concessions and became hostile to Catholics. In retaliation, the area now known as Danang was seized by the French in August 1858, launching an era of occupation that was to last for close to a century. Saigon was captured in 1861 and the rest of the south followed six years later. Vietnam's independence ended in 1883 when French control was extended to the north. Central and north Vietnam became French protectorates, although the emperor in Hue remained nominally in power.

An old map of Southeast Asia (top left) captures the days of French colonial rule when the south was annexed as Cochinchina, the centre was renamed Annam and the north was known as Tonkin. Although French rule was fiercely resisted (top right, above), the later Nguyen emperors, who wielded nominal power in Hue, were not averse to French influences. Emperor Khai Dinh's tomb (top right, below) boasts a life-sized bronze statue made in France in 1922.

French efforts to develop the country did not alter the desire of the Vietnamese to restore their independence. Several revolts in the late 19th century were unsuccessful in reviving self-rule. Out of these tumultuous times was born the communist party led by Ho Chi Minh.

When France fell to Nazi Germany in 1940, an agreement was made to accept the presence of Japanese troops (who were Germany's ally) in Vietnam. The Japanese however left the routine administration of the country to the French. It was not until 1945 that the Japanese overthrew the French in favour of a puppet regime led by the last of the Nguyen emperors, Bao Dai.

Ho Chi Minh, in the meantime, had succeeded in welding several disaffected communist groups into a single entity popularly known as the Viet Minh. He was quick to capitalise on the political power vacuum created by the defeat of the Japanese in World War II. The Viet Minh won complete control of the north while Emperor Bao Dai, aware of the broad-based support for Ho, abdicated in central Vietnam. In the south, the revolutionaries formed a shaky coalition with non-communist groups. The Vietnamese nation was declared an independent republic by President Ho Chi Minh on 2 September 1945.

Amidst political confusion, negotiations with France on the future of Vietnam proved fruitless. Skirmishes culminated in the shelling of the northern port of Haiphong, where hundreds of civilians were killed. The Franco-Viet Minh war, which lasted almost a decade, broke out in Hanoi at the end of 1946.

The century-old French rule finally ended in 1954 at Dien Bien Phu, a valley near the Laotian border. The Viet Minhs had hauled heavy artillery to the top of the steep hills surrounding the valley, something the French had thought impossible. The surrender of more than 10,000 starving French troops in a 57-day siege effectively ended French public support of the war. Soon after, the Geneva Accords was signed, providing for the exchange of prisoners, the temporary division of Vietnam into two zones near the 17th parallel at Ben Hai River, the free passage of people across the 17th parallel for 300 days and the holding of nationwide elections in 1956.

Ironically, the Vietnamese lost their unity upon gaining full national independence. The North was ruled by the communist party under Ho Chi Minh while the South was led by the fiercely anti-communist Catholic, Ngo Dinh Diem, with strong support from the Americans. The two Vietnams had no diplomatic, cultural or commercial relations with each other. Elections, called for in the Geneva Accords, were never held and they existed in a virtual state of war.

Diem's repressive regime, initially tolerated by his supporters, received worldwide condemnation when a protesting Buddhist monk set himself on fire. The US backed a coup in which Diem was assassinated and conflict escalated. Troops from the north were covertly dispatched to join their brothers in the south, popularly known as Viet Cong, via the Ho Chi Minh trail through the mountains. The Americans beefed up their military presence to counter the Viet Cong threat, and the French-Indochina War against the colonialists was now replaced by an anti-communist crusade.

The war with America and her allies lasted for a decade during which the forces of the superpower were constantly frustrated by the guerrilla tactics employed by the Viet Cong. The guerrillas would strike, then disappear into vast networks of underground tunnels to blend with the local community. The Tet Offensive, launched on the eve of the Vietnamese New Year by communist troops, sealed the fate of this war.

Though the casualty rates among Viet Congs and civilians were high, television coverage of the event shocked the American public. Anti-war sentiments finally forced the withdrawal of American troops. The South, economically devastated by the withdrawal, surrendered to the North. Vietnam was finally unified.

Vietnam's history is one of struggle; a struggle for national pride and independence. War is seldom heroic, but the Vietnamese have emerged from theirs with a dignity and grace peculiar perhaps to an ancient civilisation with a rich culture.

The defeat of the militarily more powerful French and Americans was possible only because Ho Chi Minh (top) enjoyed popular support. This support is still evident 30 years after his death as army relics to his memory, such as those kept in Hanoi's Flag Tower (bottom), are also found on street posters.

PART ONE

THE LAND

Vietnam was, for decades, seen through the eyes of journalists covering the country's conflicts and war veterans at the middle of these hostilities. Inevitably, the image presented was seldom flattering. But when the first inquisitive steps were taken to assess the aftermath of a country isolated for 40 years, its beauty proved so startling that the intrepid few soon avalanched into tourist hordes. Suddenly, the world is rediscovering Vietnam's beauty—a beauty as varied as it is stunning.

This variety comes as a surprise, for Vietnam is often described as brown and green with a mass of highlands and low level plains. Though not inaccurate, the picture is misleading. A bird's eye view reveals a pretty landscape, but the rich tapestry nature bestowed on Vietnam can only be appreciated in detail. Only then will the colours present themselves in their various, if subtle, shades.

The magnificence of Fan Si Pan's white-capped peaks can be experienced on the highest point of the Hoang Lien mountain range in the northwest. In winter, it is covered by the pristine white of snow and in summer, the brilliant white of clouds. The summit overlooks the cool plateaus of the Central Highlands where the brown rocky outcrops of the Truong Son mountain range plunge into deep green valleys and give way to the dark lush greens of tropical rain forests, tea slopes and coffee plantations.

These lush greens merge with the more luminous hues of the padi fields, which stretch from the terraced central slopes to the rich alluvial plains of the Red River Delta in the northeast and the Mekong Delta in the south. The colours of this vast sea of fields are forever changing. From the brown of a muddy, flooded plot awaiting the transplanting of seedlings to the bright green of the young padi shoots, the fields turn to gold when the padi is ready for harvesting, finally returning to brown in an endless cycle of renewal.

And all this is fed by the waters which gush down in silver sheets from the mountains into shimmering waterfalls on the Central Highlands, or rivers and streams which snake their way in muddy green through the rain forests and translucent blue through villages, turning a muddy brown in the vast delta plains to meet the sea. On the coast, which stretches from the Gulf of Tonkin in the north to the Gulf of Thailand in the south, tree-lined white beaches with luminous green waters flow into tranquil bays whose dark emerald waters lap round offshore coral islands before meeting the deep blue of the South China Sea.

Not content with the colours bestowed by nature, the Vietnamese have added to their canvas, urban landscapes of vibrant intensities. The cities of Hanoi, Hue and Ho Chi Minh City are like siblings—they come from the same womb but have different characters. Hanoi is stately, Hue is ancient and cultural while Ho Chi Minh is cosmopolitan, but their streets are never empty. The first is Vietnam's political capital, the second its last imperial outpost and the third its centre of commerce and industry, but all serve as counterpoints to the natural landscape, emphasising its beauty and diversity.

The beauty of Vietnam has not been lavished with the widespread accolades of other Asian lands like Thailand. But already, it is the Asian hotspot. As they say, beauty is eloquent even when silent.

The tranquillity of padi fields (left and above) complements the languid pace of rural life (following pages). Even the journey into the bustle of the city on market day takes on a relaxed charm (following page inset).

RIVERS OF LIFE

Rivers play an important role in the ecology and economy of any nation. More so for Vietnam, where the Red River in the north and the Mekong River in the south meet the South China Sea.

With 75% of the country covered by highlands, the rivers and their deltas are indeed the lifeline of the country. They are two of the most densely populated areas in the world. Silt from the rivers collect at the mouths, forming fertile alluvial plains. As a result, both deltas are so densely cultivated that they are known as the rice bowls of Vietnam, the third largest exporter of rice in the world.

As the river gives so the river takes. Frequent floods cause considerable damage, forcing delta dwellers to build their houses on stilts. Crops do not escape devastation. Sometimes, livestock and human lives are lost. When the waters retreat, farmers pick up their ploughs again, returning to the fields with Buddhist fatalism.

Rice Planting

An endless sea of padi fields cover the coastal regions of Vietnam. Farmers in their conical hats still cultivate their fields by wading knee-deep in water behind their buffalo-drawn ploughs, stooping in muddy waters from morn to dusk transplanting seedlings or reaping the crops with a hand-held scythe. Despite being a major rice producer, all operations on the country's padi fields, including irrigation and drainage, are still done by hand.

Frustrating to the Western motorist but charming to shutterbugs is the sight of unhusked rice spread out to dry on narrow highways. The Vietnamese motorist, however, takes this encroachment by farmers in stride. Neither motorist nor farmer has a choice. For the road is the only available space left for drying the harvest. And rice is considered god's gemstone, so much so that a child eating rice is in a divine state and is never struck.

Rice is one of Vietnam's main cash crops, but operations, even on large farms, remain mostly manual, from the transplanting of seedlings (top left) to harvesting (far left), threshing (facing page) and winnowing (above). Most of these tasks are undertaken by family members, including teenaged girls (top right). Machines (left) are rare. Even when moving among large padi fields, paddle power is employed (preceding pages).

The Mighty Mekong

It thunders down as white waters in the high plateaus of Tibet; tumbles through canyons three kilometres deep in Yunnan, China; flows into the heart of the Golden Triangle, the waters which separate Myanmar, Laos and Thailand; plunges into the jungle highlands of Laos and sweeps into Cambodia before sprawling into Vietnam. The world's twelfth longest river and the seventh longest in Asia flows 4,160 kilometres through six countries before meeting the South China Sea. Because of these countries' troubled and turbulent history, the Mekong remains one of the least developed of Asia's rivers.

The only metropolis is found at its mouth in southern Vietnam. Here, the river sprawls into the River of Nine Dragons, as it is popularly known to the Vietnamese, since it used to empty into the sea in nine tributaries. Two have silted up, but the delta waterways are home to more than a fifth of Vietnam's population.

Besides padi farms, catfish farms are also abundant. Farmers raise the freshwater fish under their floating houses, lifting a trap door in their living rooms to fatten the giant catfish for market.

A floating market in Cai Ranh (left), where a wide variety of fruit, fish and vegetables are traded from rowing boats and sampans.

Fed by the millions of cubic metres of sediment deposited by the Mekong and its tributaries, the delta is a vast alluvial plain which rarely reaches more than two metres above sea level. Delta inhabitants live on the water (left), which provides them with a means of transportation (above and top right) as well as a source for food (centre).

Vung Tau, a popular seaside resort, was once known as Cap St Jacques, the homesick Frenchman's Riviera. Today, it is a special economic zone with a thriving oil and gas industry. But it is best known as the Bay of Boats, for the many fishing vessels landing their catch for the day's market at dawn (top right) or parked on shore when not in use (centre). The beach is also where fishermen tend to their nets (left and top left) and repair their boats (right).

The Perfume River

In the days of the Nguyen emperors, courtesans drifted up and down the Perfume River in semi-covered barges on moonlit nights, enticing rich mandarins with their beautiful voices. Now, tourists reign, cruising the river to soak in the tranquillity and marvel at the splendid royal tombs of the most beautiful city in Vietnam.

The river bisects Hue, the old imperial capital of Vietnam, into two contrasting facades. On its left bank are the remains of the moated citadel enclosing the palaces, temples and gardens of the Imperial City. On its right is the "new city", with its network of spacious tree-lined streets and colonial villas, smacking of a run-down French town.

The river of two faces tells the story of Vietnam. Of its duality and its fluidity. The old and the new. The fierce guarding of her identity and the seamless fusion of other cultures.

The poetic beauty of the Perfume River (above and facing page) was not lost on the Nguyen emperors who not only moved their capital to Hue, but also left a legacy of Chinese-inspired landmarks on the banks of the river (top, left and far left).

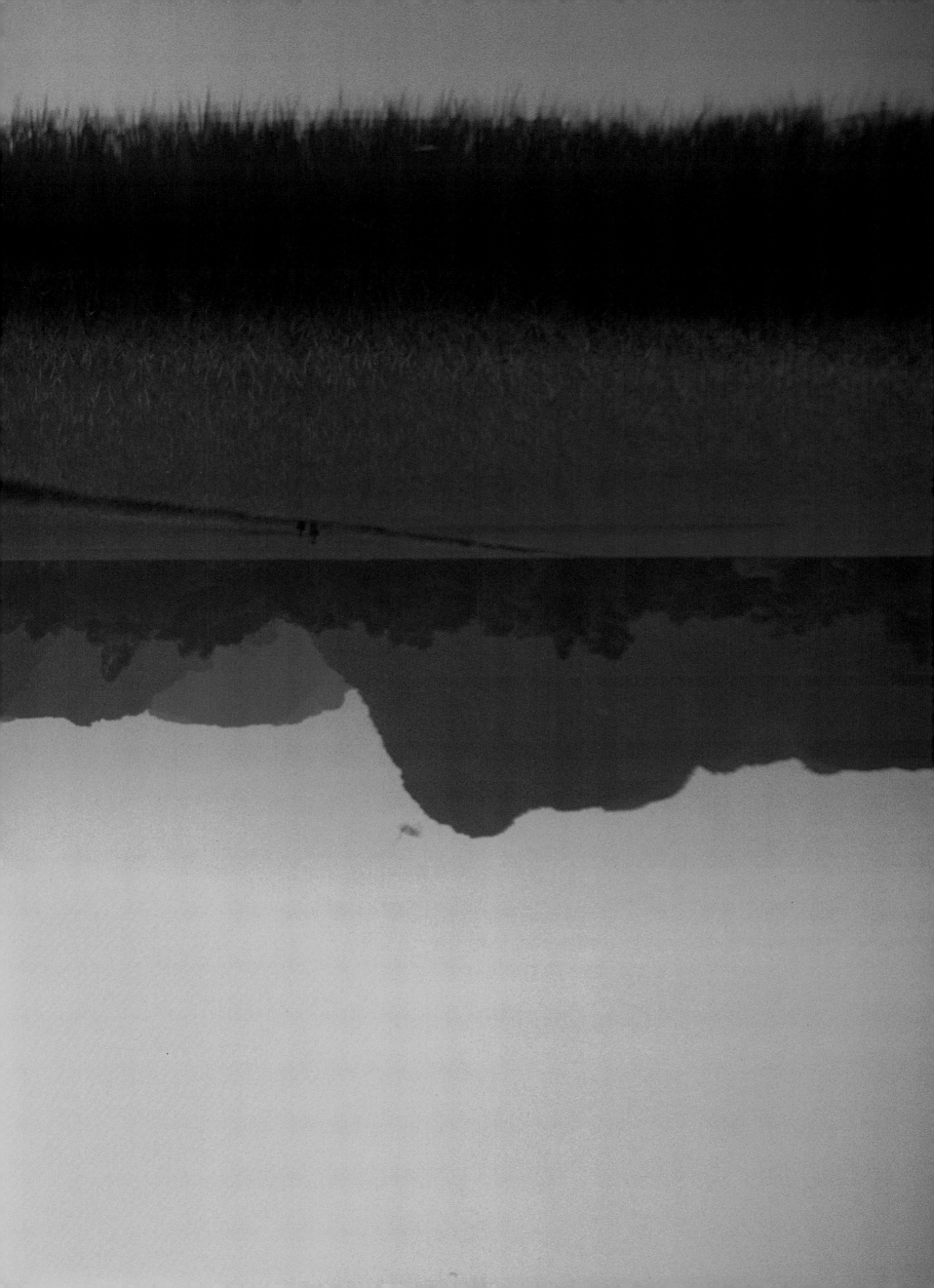

MAJESTIC MOUNTAINS

The natural beauty of Vietnam is made more staggering by the mountains and hills which cover three-quarters of her land. The highest peak, Fan Si Pan, is also the tallest in Indochina. Rising 3,160 metres in the northern mountain range of Hoang Lien, the white spurs of these mountains during frosty winters prompted homesick Europeans to christen it the Alps of Tonkin.

Less romantically looked upon but no less imposing are the mountains of Troung Son in the Central Highlands. The slopes of the mountains are covered by tropical rain forests rich in timber, medicinal plants, birds and animals. Amidst the rocky outcrops, weathered plateaus and green valleys, the ethnic minorities of Vietnam live, leading a life as hardy as the mountains on which they were born.

*T*ranquil valleys (preceding pages, main picture) and terraced fields (preceding page, bottom inset) contrast with the conditions of the mountains. While the former are fertile grounds (facing page and top right), with farmers producing enough not only for consumption but also for sale (above), farming is a subsistence activity in the highlands (right). Here, families supplement their income by making handicraft for sale (left) to tourists visiting the many scenic spots in the highlands (preceding page, top inset). Life is hard, even for the little girl who baby-sits a brother not much younger than herself (top left).

Cupid in the Clouds

Nestled on a plateau of the Hoang Lien Son mountain range is Sapa, a beautiful hill station established by the French in 1922. Minorities from the surrounding villages, dressed in their colourful costumes, congregate here every Saturday to market ethnic handicraft and products from across the Chinese border. The journey to the market is an arduous one for some. Balancing their ware in bamboo baskets, they trek through a series of mountains and valleys to reach the station, which sits at an altitude of 1,500 metres above sea level.

The eagerness with which the youngsters await the arrival of market day is not simply economic. For Sapa is also known as "Love Market". If a female Montagnard allows her male counterpart to remove any of her ornaments, it is a sign that she is willing to spend the night with him.

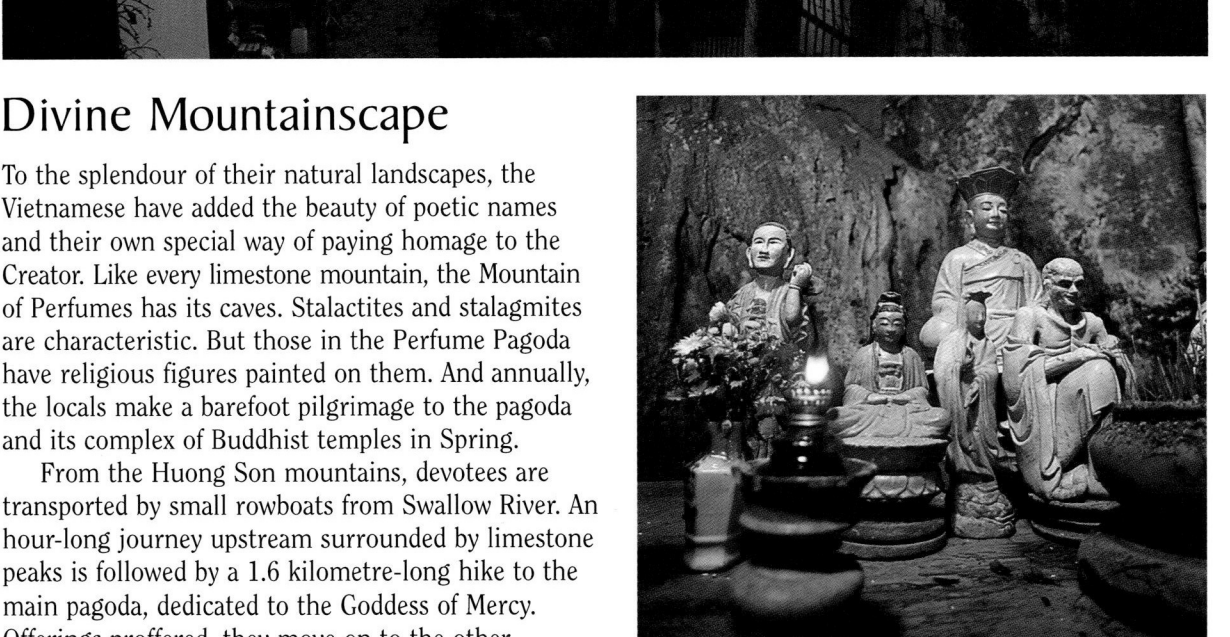

Divine Mountainscape

To the splendour of their natural landscapes, the Vietnamese have added the beauty of poetic names and their own special way of paying homage to the Creator. Like every limestone mountain, the Mountain of Perfumes has its caves. Stalactites and stalagmites are characteristic. But those in the Perfume Pagoda have religious figures painted on them. And annually, the locals make a barefoot pilgrimage to the pagoda and its complex of Buddhist temples in Spring.

From the Huong Son mountains, devotees are transported by small rowboats from Swallow River. An hour-long journey upstream surrounded by limestone peaks is followed by a 1.6 kilometre-long hike to the main pagoda, dedicated to the Goddess of Mercy. Offerings proffered, they move on to the other grottoes, believed to be inhabited by deities with healing powers.

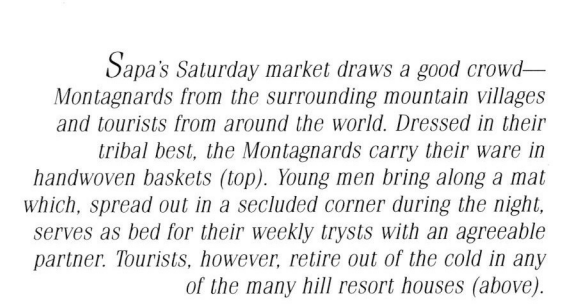

Sapa's Saturday market draws a good crowd—Montagnards from the surrounding mountain villages and tourists from around the world. Dressed in their tribal best, the Montagnards carry their ware in handwoven baskets (top). Young men bring along a mat which, spread out in a secluded corner during the night, serves as bed for their weekly trysts with an agreeable partner. Tourists, however, retire out of the cold in any of the many hill resort houses (above).

As many as 30,000 people visit the Perfume Pagoda each day during the peak Spring season (left). Devotees enjoy a scenic boat ride from the Swallow River (below top), then trek uphill (below centre), some barefooted, before reaching the pagoda where offerings are made (below bottom).Other picturesque mountain caves where the Vietnamese worship include the Marble Mountain (facing page, second from bottom), once a Viet Cong sanctuary, and the Grotto That Swallows the Cloud (facing page, bottom).

37

THE ISLANDS AND COASTS

Surrounded by seas in the east, south and southwest, Vietnam has a coastline of 3,260 kilometres. This lengthy coastline has resulted in a variety of landscapes, contributing to the diversity of the country's beauty.

There are dank and dark mangrove swamps infested with crocodiles and leeches and reputedly, ghosts and spirits. There are beautiful coves and poetic bays formed when dragons protected the good and innocent. There are sheer cliffs and treacherous waters which even the most adventurous will avoid. And there are stretches of pristine white beaches with sand dunes that rise 40 metres high.

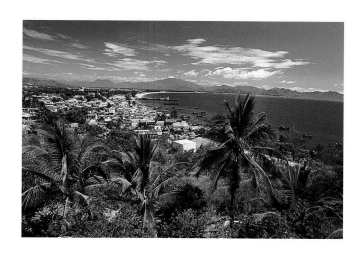

Situated on the edge of the Pacific Ocean's storm basin, typhoons batter Vietnam's shores every year, causing considerable loss and damage (right).

Vietnam's lengthy coastline boasts beautiful coves (top) and poetic bays, the most well-known being Halong Bay (following page, bottom inset), considered by some to be the most beautiful stretch of waters in the world. This perception is no doubt reinforced by the charming sight of traditional stiff-sailed junks (following page, top inset) navigated with ease by fishermen in these parts. Elsewhere, fishing is done on more conventional vessels (facing page). Offering unique water transport between shore and larger vessels are bucket boats (above and far left), while visitors island hop in more comfort on regular water taxis (following pages).

Halong Bay
—The Inspiration of Poets

Several versions of its origins, all related to the dragon, exist. One legend tells of how the mythological animal, when returning from heaven to its watery home, left such deep foot imprints that valleys were formed. When it plunged into the water, the sea rose, flooding these valleys and turning the surrounding mountaintops into thousands of tiny islands.

All of Vietnam can rattle off at least two versions of this legend. The less romantic will insist that the hundreds of tiny, craggy islands jutting out from the sea were once limestone mountains which eroded with the passage of time. But the fact remains that Halong Bay is a scenic wonder of 1,600 islands, some named after the shapes they resemble.

The largest of these is Poetry Rock, for centuries a refuge to scholars seeking inspiration. Bandits of yore too sought cover in the many uninhabited caves and to this day, fishermen catching forty winks or sheltering from a sudden thunderstorm do so in some of the caves.

URBAN LANDSCAPES
— A TALE OF THREE CITIES

Thailand has Bangkok and the Philippines has Manila. But Vietnam has Hanoi, Hue and Ho Chi Minh City. Hanoi has served as the political capital from earliest history, Hue was the imperial capital of the country's last emperor, Saigon was the southern capital when Vietnam was divided and now as Ho Chi Minh City, is the focus of commerce and industry.

The country's political history has made it necessary to speak of them in one breath.

At the same time, they are as different as siblings born and bred in the same family can be. Ho Chi Minh City is brash, pursuing bright lights and modern conveniences, including Vietnam's first family entertainment complex comprising shops, a supermarket, food court, video arcade, billiard saloon and bowling alley, Hanoi, a city of lakes and trees, is less noisy, polluted and crowded, ever the more sedate older brother. Hue, well known for the beauty of its landscape and its women, is the poetic and artistic younger sister.

And like a family, they co-exist in harmony, never detracting from the whole. Rather they add another dimension to the rich tapestry of Vietnam's landscape.

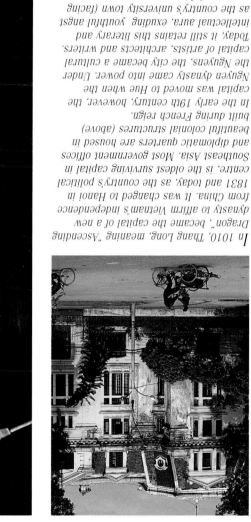

In 1010, Thang Long, meaning "Ascending Dragon", became the capital of a new dynasty to affirm Vietnam's independence from China. It was changed to Hanoi in 1831 and today, as the country's political centre, is the oldest surviving capital in Southeast Asia. Most government offices and diplomatic quarters are housed in beautiful colonial structures (above) built during French reign.

In the early 19th century, however, the capital was moved to Hue when the Nguyen dynasty came into power. Under the Nguyens, the city became a cultural capital of artists, architects and writers. Today, it still retains this literary and intellectual aura, exuding youthful angst as the country's university town (facing page, top left).

Ho Chi Minh City, still referred to by many as Saigon, sits on the banks of the Saigon River (above). True to its reputation as the city of commerce and industry, its streets are never empty (below right). And in this country of bicycles and Honda cubs, cars—a rare sight in the provinces— are not uncommon on its wide boulevards (facing page, top right).

The devastation suffered in several wars is a memory not easily forgotten. Artillery shells are found not only in war museums but also among ruins (bottom right). The Cu Chi Tunnel, a brilliant Vietnamese strategy against their better equipped French and American enemies, is open to the public, if only in parts (below left and centre). And to remind future generations of their hard-earned independence, busts of Ho Chi Minh (following pages) by sculptor Diep Minh Chan are cast for posterity.

Vestiges of War

Vietnamese schoolchildren listen in awe as their teachers point to the spot where their patriotic granduncles emerged under the cover of night through a wooden trapdoor on another mission to frustrate the enemy. Those who wish may join the camera-slinging tourists for a spell underground. But although this section of the Cu Chi Tunnel has been enlarged and upgraded, few linger. How the guerrillas lived for days, even months, in these claustrophobic passages and chambers baffle not only the Americans with whom they fought several decades ago.

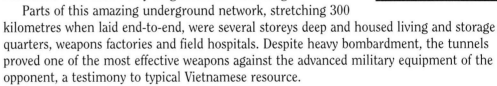

Parts of this amazing underground network, stretching 300 kilometres when laid end-to-end, were several storeys deep and housed living and storage quarters, weapons factories and field hospitals. Despite heavy bombardment, the tunnels proved one of the most effective weapons against the advanced military equipment of the opponent, a testimony to typical Vietnamese resource.

PART TWO
FLORA AND FAUNA

Much of Vietnam used to be covered in dense forests. With civilisation came a progressive destruction of these forests for cultivation of crops such as padi, especially in the coastal and low-lying regions. But the real carnage to Vietnamese flora and fauna occurred during the Vietnam War, when the Americans employed ecocide in an ineffective attempt to flush out the Viet Congs.

Millions of litres of herbicide were sprayed to strip the trees of their leaves; bulldozers were used in land clearing operations to flatten large tracts of forests; and canals were dug to drain the swamps. Even wildlife, specifically the elephant, were bombed or napalmed from the air to decimate the limited means of transport for the militarily less equipped Vietnamese. It has been estimated that the deforestation caused then would have supplied the country with timber for 30 years. And besides elephants, a great variety of wildlife perished with the forests.

Today, only two-fifths of the country is covered by woodlands. Long after the war, Vietnam is still suffering from the effects of chemical warfare. The once abundant Sarich Crane, for example, is now close to extinction.

But as if competing with the people of Vietnam for resilience, her forests are still home to 12,000 plant species with 7,000 identified and 2,300 useful to humans as medicine, food, animal fodder and wood products. Its wide range of habitats, ranging from equatorial lowlands to temperate highlands, boast 200 species of mammals, 800 species of birds, 100 species of amphibians, 150 species of reptiles and 1,000 species of marine life.

Even more remarkable is the discovery of hitherto unknown fauna. The world's last species of land mammal was found 50 years ago. But in 1992, a previously unknown species of forest goat was found in the isolated Vu Quang Nature Reserve in North Vietnam. The goat was only the fourth large land mammal to be discovered in the 20th century. Two years later, a species of barking deer was discovered near the same site. Likewise, the Eastern Saurus Crane was found in Tram Chim in the Mekong Delta in 1986, the first time that it has been found outside its breeding ground in Cambodia.

Because Vietnam has suffered much ecological devastation, the diversity of her flora and fauna proves surprising. Whereas man has wrought destruction, nature has blessed her with a climate conducive to the propagation of the rain forest, a veritable ecosystem which maintains the survival of the smallest bug to the biggest mammal and ground level creepers to canopy foliage.

Valiant attempts are also being made to protect and restore the country's diverse flora and fauna. Nine thousand hectares in Tram Chim have been set aside as a reserve for the Eastern Saurus Crane. An active programme to replant the country with 500 million trees is also underway. Replanted forests however, still suffering from the devastating effects of the herbicide Agent Orange, remain sparse although some wildlife such as birds and fish have reappeared in replanted mangrove swamps.

Vietnam's flora and fauna will never be restored to their original state. But her regreening programme, if pursued with the same relentlessness displayed in her struggle for independence, will one day lead to a more balanced ecosystem.

Idyllic scenes of contented fauna (left) and bountiful flora (above) belie the fact that Vietnam, the first country subject to major ecological warfare, is still struggling to recover from the devastating environmental damage sustained.

NATURAL RICHES OF
A PLUNDERED LAND

I n the light of the devastation sustained through war and progress, Vietnam's flora and fauna seems impressive. In addition to the rain forests which cover two-fifths of the land, the high plateaus are home to plantations of tea, coffee, vegetables and flowers. The sedimentary volcanic lands found in the lower deltas are used for pepper and rubber cultivation while the rich alluvial plains produce an abundance of rice and a variety of tropical fruits including longan, mango, guava and jackfruit.

Wildlife, though only a shadow of what it used to be, still boasts some of the great species of the world such as the elephant, panther, tiger and bear. Forests also teem with deer, birds and hare, while swamps breed crocodiles and snakes. Freshwater fish like carp and the giant catfish live in the numerous lakes, rivers, and even flooded rice fields, while crayfish and eel are common catch.

Elephants were bombed from the air in an attempt by the Americans to destroy the limited means of transport for the Vietnamese guerrillas. In the process, other flora and fauna were decimated. Today, fauna such as elephants (far right) and deer (below), just beginning to recover from the last devastation in the sparsely populated highlands (above), face another breed of enemies. Gun-toting poachers hunt elephants for their tusks and deer for their horns, meat and pelts.

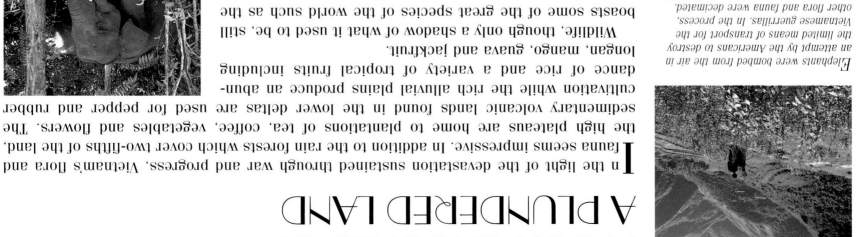

Hunters of Vietnam

Their forefathers supplemented their diet of slash-and-burn agricultural crops like maize with meat hunted in forests. This ancient way of life is still practised by many Montagnard tribes such as the Thai, Hmong, Dao and Muong. The Muongs living in the Cuc Phuong National Park still hunt with blowpipes but some, like the Hmongs, use weapons left over from the war.

The destructive aspect of hunting came about with progress. Royalty delighted in hunting as sport. One of the most celebrated hunters must be Bao Dai, the last emperor of Vietnam. Despite a forced abdication from the throne, he continued his luxurious lifestyle, indulging his love of the sport through long hunting expeditions in the Central Highlands, using as many as 20 elephants to encircle his prey.

Today, animals are no longer hunted purely for food or pleasure. Poachers engage in the illegal activity for commercial gain. Elephants, wild cats, monkeys, even snakes are not spared. Some are captured alive, others are shot on sight but they end up as exotic food, medicine or ornament to those who can afford them.

Animal Sacrifice

Meat, especially chicken, fish and pork are offered as sacrifice to one's ancestors. Buffaloes are slain to appease the gods, thereby ensuring a good harvest. But like many other Asian countries, Vietnam's more exotic wildlife fall prey to the palates of the Chinese.

Frogs, turtles, pangolins, bats, pythons and cobras are just some of the delicacies offered. Snakes, in fact, have proven so lucrative that entrepreneurial Vietnamese are cultivating them on farms. Their skins are used for handbags, belts and wallets; their bones dried and used for the manufacture of gelatine; and their flesh used as feed for animals or food for humans. Snake wine is believed to invigorate; snake oil cures aches and pain; and snake cream is used in cosmetics.

But it is the large land mammals which, already dwindling from the shrinkage of their natural habitat, are further decimated by poachers who hunt them for short-term gain. Elephants are prized for their ivory. Tigers are sought after as their bones are believed to cure backache and their pelts are fashion accessories. The antlers of deer, gall of bears and civets, and bones of monkeys are all believed to have medicinal qualities.

Their forefathers hunted if they needed meat, but nowadays, meat is readily available in the market (centre). Pig rearing is a lucrative business but even more so is snake farming. Every part of the reptile, from its bones to its skin, has a commercial value. Many Vietnamese men also swear by the invigorating qualities of snake wine (above).

A Day at the Races

Horseracing used to be a favourite pastime among the French in Vietnam. The cultured denizens of the Hippodrome at Phu Tho were replaced by rich ethnic Chinese from Cholon when the country gained independence in 1954. When Saigon fell to the communists in 1975, the authorities banned horseracing as a bourgeois indulgence. It was not until 1990 that the racetracks came to life again.

Today, horseracing is one of the few activities in Vietnam enjoyed as a mass spectator sport. Renamed the Phu Tho Racecourse, the grounds are open every weekend. Among the gamblers and spectators are children—some on a day out with their parents, others selling food and drinks. And still others, in jockey garb, hold the reins to many a hardcore gambler's dreams. For Vietnam is one of the few places in the world where children, between the ages of 10 and 15, are allowed as jockeys.

Horses are bred not only for domestic use in the highlands. In resorts such as Dalat's Valley of Love, once the hunting ground of Emperor Bao Dai and now the haunt of lovers and honeymooning couples, horseback riding is popular. There, local tourists, many of them urban dwellers, do not mind paying the suitably-clad horse minders (left and top right) for that once in a lifetime ride.
Paid to ride are the jockeys at the Phu Tho Racecourse (above). Aged between 10 and 15, these lightweight boys make the equivalent of a working adult's monthly salary in a day if they ride a winner.

BIRDWATCHER'S PARADISE

Vietnam, with its spectacular variety of birds, is a birdwatcher's paradise. Out of the 800 species of birds found here, 9 are endemic and 33 others, although also found elsewhere, are threatened by extinction. Most of the endemic birds are found in the highlands, while Chinese and Burmese birds are found in the lowlands.

Common birds include Spotted Doves, Red-whiskered Bulbuls and White-rumped Munias. Rare ones are the Imperial Pheasants and Pale-capped Pigeon, while the Black-hooded Laughing Thrush can only be found in Vietnam.

With a diversity of habitats ranging from equatorial lowlands to temperate highlands, Vietnam is blessed with a bird fauna that is unusually varied. The Red-Whiskered Bulbul (main picture) is a resident of the country while other common species include (clockwise from top left) the Hobbed Pitta, Spotted Munia, Spotted Dove, Collared Kingfisher, Lesser Treeduck and White-Throated Kingfisher.

CREATURES OF THE SEA AND COAST

The significance of the sea to the Vietnamese is understandable when one realises the importance of *nuoc mam*, or fish sauce, to their diet. But fish is not the only spectacular aquatic creature of the country's 1,000 species of marine life.

On the coasts, aquatic birds such as ducks, kingfishers and herons are common. In the freshwater lakes, carp and giant catfish abound. And in the ocean, corals and a teeming marine life add colour and diversity to the flora and fauna on land.

Low density fishing and unexplored wrecks from the war, coupled by its rugged coastline and a proliferation of islands, make Vietnam a diver's dream. Steep rock formations and vertical coral reefs are complemented by the presence of pelagic fish such as mantas, sharks and jacks.

The Origin of the Sand Crab

A Vietnamese legend says that the crab is actually the soul of a man. Blessed with a precious pearl which was kept in his mouth, the man could understand the conversations conducted in the animal kingdom. One day, while making a trip on the ocean, he chanced upon some squids singing. The sound so tickled him that he laughed out loud, dropping the pearl in the process. He spent the rest of his life sifting through the sand looking for his magical pearl. When he died, his soul became a sand crab, still turning over the sand in an endless bid to find the precious pearl.

Following pages: Much of Vietnam's flora and fauna has been destroyed by wars and population growth. But with the identification of more sites as protected national parks and a concerted effort to protect the natural habitats of jungle dwellers, environmentalists are hopeful that wildlife, such as the long-tailed macaques, would once again flourish in the forests.

The waters around Vietnam teem with life, providing gainful employment for entire families. The day's catch is sorted and cleaned by coastal dwellers (facing page and left) before being sold in the market or city streets (above).
Although marine life is still plentiful, there are fears that it may deteriorate from careless commercial plundering. Lobsters (top left) are prized catch to satiate the demands of tourist palates while corals (top right) have been dredged from colourful reefs to be sold as souvenirs.

Temple of the Whale God

In the village *dinh* of Cua Be, a temple has been consecrated to the whale god, or *Ong Nam Hai*. It is believed that before Gia Long became emperor, a whale saved his junk from being shipwrecked. When he ascended the throne, he ordered temples to be built in its honour. So revered were they that whenever a dead whale washed up on a beach, the government would donate red silk for its burial. The bones of the whales were subsequently kept in these temples.

Vietnamese fishermen believe that whales rule the sea. These lords of the sea would rescue boats in peril or capsize ships when offended. Every year, therefore, fishermen from neighbouring villages gather at Cua Be for a three-day ceremony in honour of the whale god.

NATIONAL PARKS

Vietnam has some of the world's most picturesque national parks. The first was discovered in 1960 and given protected status in 1966. The Cuc Phuong National Park sits on 25,000 hectares of land in a large valley protected by limestone mountains which reach 400 metres high. Among its 2,000 species of flora are 1,000-year-old trees which grow to heights of 50 metres. Tigers, spotted deer, monkeys and birds are some of the wildlife roaming the forests.

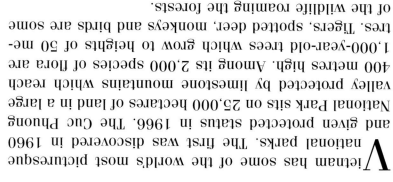

Equally scenic but more easily accessible is the Cat Ba National Park. Sited on a 600-hectare island, it boasts a range of different ecosystems including forested hills, sandy beaches, mangrove and freshwater swamps, lakes and waterfalls. Besides a variety of fish and coral, 600 species of plants, 21 species of birds and 28 species of mammals live here.

Vietnam has significantly less national parks and nature reserves than ecologists would hope for but the situation is slowly changing. Hoping to prevent the 54 species of mammals and 60 species of birds on their endangered list from becoming extinct like the tapir and the Sumatran rhinoceros, the government has identified 87 more sites for protection, with 37 already approved.

MYTHICAL ANIMALS

Their belief that the world is governed by gods and spirits explains the abundance of Vietnamese myths. In many of them, animals take centrestage.

The dragon features prominently in historical legends. As sons of the dragon king, there is a natural affinity between the Vietnamese and this mythical lord of the animal kingdom. The scenic beauty of Halong Bay is attributed to it. The robes of emperors are adorned with it. On important occasions such as the official opening of a new business, dragon dancers are necessary as the new venture's performance depended on it.

Synonymous with luck and power, the dragon is used as an architectural motif under eaves and gables and on the corners of temples and pagodas. Incense burners use dragon heads as handles. The mythical animal coils languidly round pillars, guards pagoda gates with confidence, or adorn the balustrades of temple steps with majesty.

The tortoise is another animal with mythical associations. Although not as revered as the dragon, its contribution to history was significant enough for a pagoda in the heart of Hanoi to be dedicated to it. On an island in the middle of *Ho Hoan Kiem*, or Lake of Restored Sword, stands the three-storey Tortoise Pagoda, a tribute to the animal for helping the Vietnamese gain independence from the Chinese. A symbol of longevity, the tortoise is also immortalised in Hanoi's Temple of Literature, where 82 stelae rest on the backs of stone tortoises.

The belief that they are descended from the dragon king explains the recurrence of the mythical animal as a recurring motif in Vietnamese decorative art. The power of the dragon is often captured in stone and the sculpture strategically placed at entrances (left) or roof tops (right centre) of buildings to guard its inhabitants from potential danger.
The feminine counterpart of the dragon is the phoenix. This symbol of beauty is never cast in stone, but always in a material such as ivory and gold (above), more suited to its elegant form.

Not only are mythical animals imbued with special powers, all living things, the Vietnamese believe, have spirits which can be harnessed for human good. The strength and loyalty of the elephant is useful in guarding abodes (left) while the tortoise (below) is a symbol of longevity. The resource of the lion makes it another suitable guardian (above top). Lions, like dragons, also make an appearance during auspicious occasions such as Tet, temple consecrations or the official opening of new businesses when acrobatic or martial arts troupes are engaged to perform rousing dances for good luck.

PART THREE
PEOPLE, CUSTOMS AND BELIEFS

Patriotic Vietnamese will explain that their four decades of struggle for independence was based on the belief that Vietnam is one country with one people. Afterall, they are *dong bao* or born of the same womb.

It may be difficult to accept that the Vietnamese race sprang from the hundred eggs sired by the dragon lord who married the mountain princess, as locals would tell you with great conviction. But it is easy to believe that they are from the same womb. A person from Hanoi speaks the same language as another from Ho Chi Minh City and they celebrate the same major festivals as their fellowman from Hue. But peel away the veneer and a potpourri of both subtle and distinct differences—in language, customs, costumes and beliefs—greet you.

The large proportion, some 85% of the total population, of Viets or Kinhs, explains the apparent similarities. But a southerner will tell you he is more liberal, less reserved, and more fun-loving than his brothers up north while a northerner will say he is less spendthrift, more hospitable and more reliable than his countrymen down south.

The subtle differences in their attitude to life is just a little less obvious than the regional variations in their speech, although a single major language is spoken throughout Vietnam. These regional variations are accompanied by a difference in northern, central and southern accents, indistinguishable to many, but obvious to the accustomed ear.

More distinct are the variations in costume, custom and religion of the Montagnards, 54 ethnic minority tribes which live in the highlands. A woman with tattooed palms is instantly recognised as a member of the Lao tribe whereas one who wears a blouse with silver forged into butterfly buttons is a Thai. Every Montagnard village has its own gods and deities.

So too the Viet village, many of which still have their own patron deity. It comes as no surprise then that although close to 80% of the population profess to Buddhism, their religious rituals are much more diverse. Confucian and Taoist philosophies are revered as much as Buddha's teachings, and ancestor worship and animism play an important part in their spiritual lives. Vietnam is also the birthplace of one of the world's most unusual religions, Cao Dai, a fusion of various religious beliefs.

Indeed, life in Vietnam is regulated by a vast array of beliefs and taboos, which takes on a colourful verve in the celebration of customs such as Tet, the Vietnamese new year. Regardless of their religious inclination, be they Buddhists, Christians, Muslims or Cao Daists, all Vietnamese celebrate Tet with the same joy and energy. And it is occasions like Tet, with its numerous rituals and taboos, which clearly exemplify the richness of the Vietnamese culture.

The grocery merchant in Haiphong (left) will tell you with conviction that he is descended from the union of the dragon king and the mountain princess while novice monks (above) will tell you that the present is more important than the past.

62

Romantic legends notwithstanding, the physical attributes and cultural habits of the Vietnamese bear many similarities to their Chinese and Malay neighbours. The fruit seller (top), calligrapher (above), cured meat vendor (left) or young family (right) could be mistaken for the citizens of any of Vietnam's Southeast Asian neighbours.

DESCENDANTS OF THE DRAGON KING

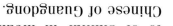

During the Stone Age, a group of adventurous southern Chinese from Guangdong province pushed southwards in search of more food. Settling in Vietnam's Red River Valley, they interbred with the earlier Malayo-Polynesian and Thai tribes. Thus was born the ethnic Viet.

Although the Viets consider themselves descendants of the dragon king, historians and anthropologists point to the similarities in the religious rites and cultural beliefs of the two communities. Even today, the Vietnamese language contains words which are close to or similar in meaning and pronunciation to the Cantonese dialect spoken by the Chinese of Guangdong.

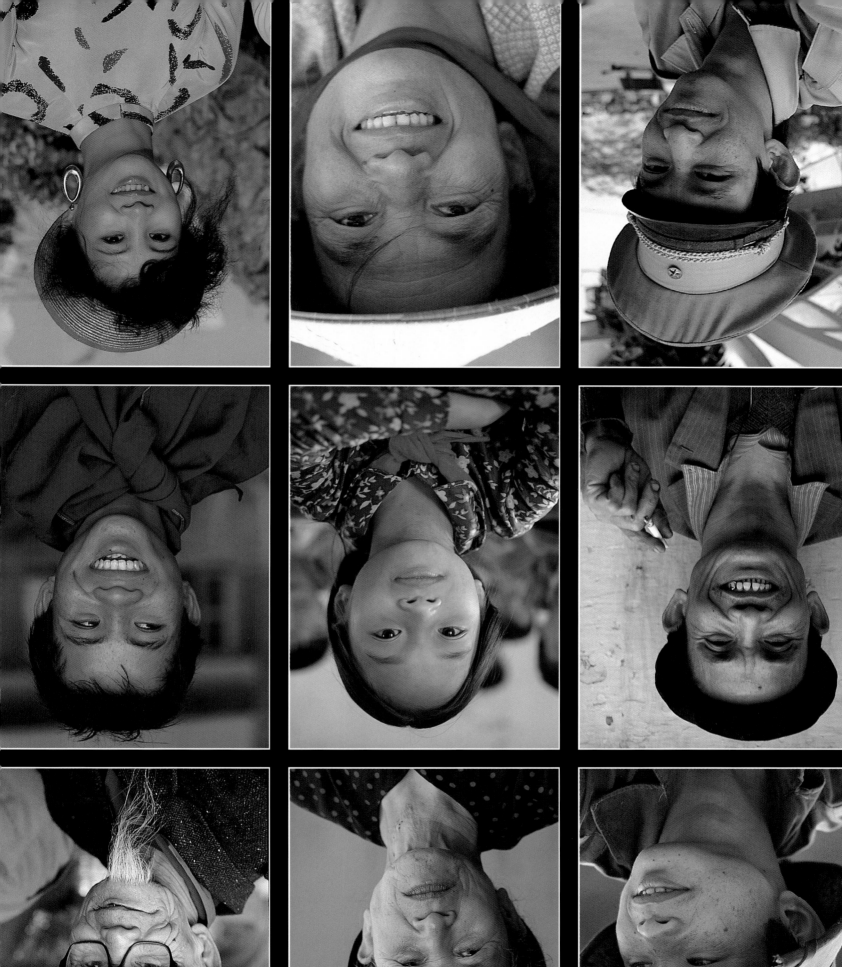

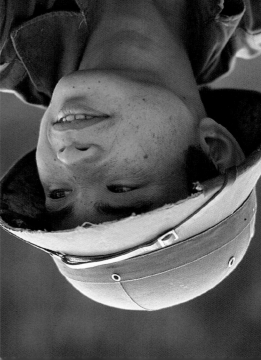

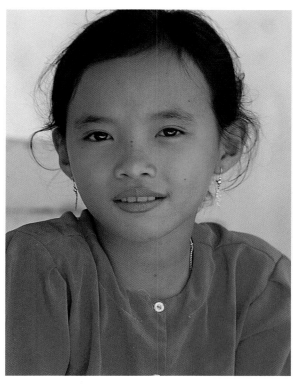

One Country, Many People

At first glance, it is easy to be convinced that Vietnam is one country with one people. The sheer number of the ethnic Viets overshadows the presence of the other minority groups, with the exception of the Montagnards, who are prominent only because their colourful costumes and customs are too difficult to ignore. The Hoas, Khmers and Chams are less easily identified.

Go to South Vietnam's Chinatown in Cholon and the shopkeeper you buy your black ebony chopsticks from speaks and looks Vietnamese. But he is likely to be a Hoa. Of Chinese origin, the Hoas are the largest ethnic minority. Although they have lived in Vietnam for generations, they still maintain the Chinese custom of organising themselves into communities based on their dialect and their ancestral province.

Likewise, the Khmer padi farmer on the Mekong Delta is like any other Vietnamese farmer. But the one whose features are rounder and darker is the Khmer, or ethnic Cambodian. Unlike the ethnic Viets who practise Mahayana Buddhism, the Khmers belong to the more orthodox Theravada Buddhist faith, which was spread to the south directly from India.

Seek a Cham in Phan Thiet, the south-central coast. He is the fisherman who supplies the essential ingredient for the region's *nuoc mam*, or fish sauce. The descendants of the once glorious Indianised kingdom of Champa still observe some traditional customs but their religion is now a modified form of Hinduism. A large number of Chams have also converted to Islam.

The faces of Vietnam (this and facing page) look the same. But those who know the country will tell you there are subtle differences which go beyond the different skin shades. There are regional variations in their speech. A northerner, for example, speaks with a different accent from his fellowman in the south. Their attitude towards life also differ, just as they have different ways of preparing similar dishes.

THE MONTAGNARDS

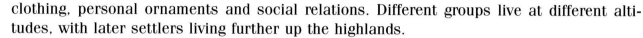

With their colourful costumes and customs, the Montagnards or highland dwellers, contribute significantly to the tapestry of Vietnamese culture. Comprising 54 ethnic groups, they live in the relatively untamed Central Highlands and northern mountains, impervious to the influence of any other culture. Ranging in size from less than 1,000 to 800,000, the larger of these groups include the Tay, Thai, Muong, Hmong, Nung, Dao, Jarai and Ede while the smaller ones are the Giay, Lao, Lu and Bo Y.

Rugged topography prevented the Montagnards living in the highlands from integrating into mainstream Vietnamese culture. Although that is slowly changing, with groups living on the lower altitudes abandoning their tribal norms by degrees, the inaccessibility of those living in the high mountains and steep valleys continue to defy the assault of lowland influences. They live just as their ancestors had done, in small cluster villages in bamboo or wooden stilt houses (top right), surviving on a low-level subsistence economy and embracing animistic beliefs.

Not only do they differ sharply from the Viet majority, they also differ from each other in language, building styles, clothing, personal ornaments and social relations. Different groups live at different altitudes, with later settlers living further up the highlands.

Identifying every one of these groups is an extremely difficult task. There is no agreement on the number of Montagnard tribes, with the figure changing according to the criteria used to differentiate them. Identification is not made easy by the fact that some groups may have more similarities than differences.

The Tays and the Nungs, for example, share the same language, culture and customs. On the other hand, the Thais can be identified as Black or White through their building styles. The former live in bamboo and stilt homes in the shape of tortoise shells while the latter live in rectangular dwellings. Then again, the same tortoise shell-shaped home can be found in a Lao village, although they are easily recognisable from the tattoos on their women's palms or their men's wrists and thighs.

These anomalies, however, only serve to make the Montagnards even more enthralling. The rugged topography of their habitat may have cut them off from mainstream Vietnamese culture but it has also contributed to a strong, resilient and fascinating race—qualities which are the essence of the Vietnamese.

Identifying the members of the different Montagnard groups is difficult for the casual observer. A Niao woman (left) is easily distinguished from the other women of the highlands (right and below) only because they are dressed in their traditional costumes. It is much harder, though, to differentiate the Meo woman (top left) from the Tay grandmother (facing page).

Like many of the larger Montagnard groups, the Hmongs (this page), are made of half a dozen subgroups. Silver is the preferred accessory, even among men. They are also known for their cultivation of poppy, from which opium is derived, for medicinal purposes.

Ho Chi Minh

He is renowned, not only in his homeland but worldwide. To his enemies, he embodied the repression of Marxist communism, a provincial boy who changed his name as often as he changed his job. To his supporters, he was a great leader who fought selflessly for his country's freedom. But in Vietnam, he is affectionately referred to as Uncle Ho, even by those who oppose communism.

It is easy to understand why Ho Chi Minh is such a revered figure in Vietnam. Much of his life was spent in hardship, fighting for his country's independence. Not only was he selflessly dedicated to his people and country, he was also a modest man who shunned glory, comfort and ostentation. Even when he was President, he preferred a simple house to a palace. And in his will, he asked to be cremated upon his death, with his ashes buried in three portions in the north, centre and south of his beloved country.

But as if reluctant to part with him, his followers have erected a mausoleum in his memory where his body, rumoured to have decayed extensively, rests.

Boat People

They risked their lives in flimsy boats on the high seas. Some were resettled in America, Canada, Australia or France. Others lost their lives at sea from conditions their boats were never equipped to handle, malnutrition, disease or at the hands of pirates who fuelled rumours that many of these refugees carried gold ingots in their luggage.

The plight of the boat people from Vietnam haunted the world for several years until new tragedies pushed them out of mind. The first wave of boat people fled after the fall of Saigon in 1975, fearing persecution for their ties with the old regime. Despite untold dangers and a more stable political climate, they continued their unauthorised departure by sea right through the eighties. All this changed in the nineties when the Orderly Departure Programme allowed emigration so that families could be reunited.

Today, those refugees who have not been resettled have returned to Vietnam. And many who have succeeded in the West are returning as visitors or businessmen. The Viet Kieus, as they are known to their countrymen, may be happily resettled in their adopted countries, but Vietnam, the land of their forefathers, is still dear to most.

Affectionately referred to as Uncle Ho, the father of independent Vietnam, Ho Chi Minh is still widely revered in his homeland (insets, top). He did not live to witness the reunification of the north and the south in 1975, which ironically, was the catalyst for the first wave of boat people (above), many of whom ended up in refugee camps (left and right).

LAND OF MANY GODS

I f embracing Marxist philosophy goes hand in hand with atheism, the guru of communism would have been sorely disappointed in Vietnam. Not only is the religious climate active, it is also very colourful.

To the Vietnamese, religion governed life before birth and well beyond the grave. Which explains the popularity of animism and ancestor worship and the abundance of myths and legends, beliefs and taboos.

Some beliefs and traditions, like Tet, is shared by all Vietnamese. Some, like the many taboos observed by fishermen, are specific to the group. Still others, like the legends of the dragon, have become so much a part of the country's culture.

So even Marx would not be surprised to find that Vietnam's main religion is a fusion of Buddhism, Confucianism and Taoism with animism and ancestor worship. Or that Cao Dai, the indigenous Vietnamese religion, merges even more religious strands under one roof. And that other religions such as Christianity, Islam, Hinduism and Hoa Hao exist to add even more colour to Vietnam's interesting kaleidoscope of beliefs.

Close to 80 per cent of Vietnam's population profess to Buddhism, which explains the predominance of Buddhist places of worship all over the country (left, above, right and below). Theravada Buddhism was introduced via trade links with India while Mahayana Buddhism came with Chinese conquest.

Although a majority of Vietnamese claim to be Buddhists, they also practise Confucianism, Taoism, animism and ancestor worship. It is therefore not uncommon to find temples with monks from various sects (above and following pages). Devotees pray not only to their dead ancestors but other deities as well (far left). Village festivals, with offerings made to the spirits of real or legendary heroes are rife (left). Christianity, and specifically Roman Catholicism, is the second major religion. Even though Vietnam's Christians worship in churches (above top), many are not averse to the practice of ancestor worship.

Followers of the Cao Dai sect wear white robes (above, right, far right and top left) while priests wear robes of yellow, red (centre right) and blue representing Buddhism, Confucianism and Taoism respectively. Strict adherence to the priests' directives is required of followers.

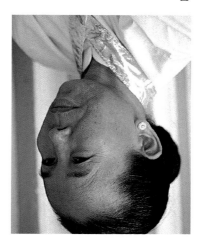

Cao Dai

Author Graham Greene once considered becoming a Cao Daist. He thought better of it, but was fascinated enough to include it in his book, *The Quiet American.*

Founded after a seance in the Mekong Delta by an obscure official working for the French, it is an amalgam of many beliefs. The Holy See, the main temple of the religion which houses the many gods and saints revered, is aptly described by Greene as "a Walt Disney fantasia of the East".

Christ and Buddha, Victor Hugo and Sun Yat Sen and a host of other gods and philosophers adorn the roof and walls of the temple. Huge pillars entwined by dragons and cobras guard the hall of worship and main entrance. Worshippers in white robes mingle with priests dressed in yellow, red and blue. Overlooking everything and everyone is the divine eye, the symbol of the religion. It's like stepping into a surreal world.

Depending on your personal beliefs and conviction, Cao Daism will awe you with its pageantry or irritate you with its pomposity. But it will surely impress you with its diversity. The colours, images and symbols are visual assaults which are not easily forgotten.

Hoa Hao

Lacking the grand trappings of Cao Dai, Hoa Hao—another indigenous Vietnamese religion founded in the south—does not excite as much curiosity and wonder.

But that is a deliberate move by its founder, whose calling was no less dramatic than that of the Cao Dai leader. Miraculously cured from a lifetime of sickness, Huynh Phu So, who studied under a famous occultist, emerged from a trance one stormy night to proclaim himself the founder of Buddhist Hoa Hao.

Instead of an elaborate temple with a rigid religious hierarchy, he preached on street corners and canal intersections, stressing a return to purity and simplicity through prayer, meditation and fasting. Only Buddha, ancestors and national heroes deserved the worship of a Hoa Hao.

They both had dramatic beginnings and became major military forces during Vietnam's period of turbulence. They also share some of the same gods. But the similarities end there.
Members of the Hoa Hao sect embrace simplicity (above), striving to attain purity through prayer, meditation and fasting.
A Cao Dai gathering, on the other hand, is a riot of colours and ceremony (facing page, centre left). While the former has no religious hierarchy, the latter is governed by a strict religious order, with authority vested in the pope and trickling down to its followers through priests and mediums.

Animism and Spiritualism

In death, one passed on into another life and in life, one is surrounded by the spirits of the dead. These spirits may be benevolent or malevolent, but they are everywhere—in the earth, trees, stones, mountains, rivers, even in the air. The Vietnamese culture is rich in tradition and religious rites precisely because of this belief that the world is inhabited by gods and spirits.

Every farmer has an altar outside his door dedicated to the earth god. Village trees harbour spirits. Mountains have caves devoted to various gods, including Goddess of Mercy, Kuan Yin and the Virgin Mary. Boat prows have eyes for the water spirits. And spirit houses dot roadsides.

These spirits can protect and help but should not be offended or ignored. Otherwise, they can cause all manner of disasters and unhappiness. Therefore, their goodwill should be cultivated, not trifled with. That explains the daily offering to ancestors and the existence of temples or pagodas for every imaginable spirit. But when weak humans unwittingly invite the wrath of these spirits or when their worldly concerns need divine intervention, their daily prayers may be insufficient and the ministrations of a medium, priest, or faith healer is needed. Through magic, incantations, charms and potions, these spiritual intermediaries intervene on behalf of lesser mortals, for a fee of course.

Appeasing the spirits which inhabit the earth is of paramount importance to a Vietnamese. Otherwise, misfortune may befall the family and bad luck will follow the transgressor. Farmers make offerings to the earth god for a good harvest (top left) while taxi-drivers ensure safety on the road through Buddhist amulets stuck to their dashboards (top right). Most families worship Buddha and Kuan Yin (facing and following pages) and all Vietnam provide elaborate funerals for their dead relatives to ease their passage into the netherworld (above, left and far left).

FESTIVE CELEBRATIONS

When the Vietnamese celebrate their many festivals, they are communicating with their gods, commemorating the past and praying for the future. Their festivals have a religious or cultural significance rooted in their traditions and beliefs.

The Lac Long Quan Festival, held from the first to the sixth day of the third lunar month at Binh Minh village in Ha Son Binh province, is dedicated to the legendary father of all Viets. Thanh Ming, held on the fifth day of the third lunar month, is reserved for honouring the dead. This annual ritual involves the cleaning of ancestral graveyards and the offering of food, paper money and incense to dead ancestors. All year round, there are festivals honouring the birth or death of national heroes, religious leaders or deities and spirits.

Agricultural festivals are also rife among the ethnic minorities who depend entirely on nature for their existence. These festivals celebrate the interaction between humans, nature and the supernatural. Good weather and a bountiful harvest are the raison d'etre for elaborate ceremonies and animal sacrifices.

Just as the Montagnards pray to the spirits of nature for fertile land, so the Viet farmers pray to the earth god for a good harvest. Fishermen and sailors pray to the Goddess of the Sea for safe passage. Women pray to the Goddess of Fertility for children. And children pray to their ancestors for protection. Just about everyone is involved in a religious celebration of faith.

The Trung sisters succeeded in revolting against Chinese domination, ruling for three years before being defeated by a huge Han army. To avoid torture at the hands of their enemies, they threw themselves into the Red River. However, their bravery is relived every year in a colourful celebration. As the sisters' spirits are invited to the ceremony (above), opera performers retell the story of their bravery in song (right and below right).

The incense ceremony (above top and bottom) is held at the ancient citadel of Co Loa, Vietnam's earliest capital during the Thuc dynasty. The ceremony, conducted according to Confucian precepts, used to be part of the rites that every Vietnamese king had to perform.

Tet—Celebration of a Moveable Feast

The whole of Vietnam celebrates Tet. As with the Chinese, the first day of the lunar calendar is an important traditional festival for the Vietnamese. And since the lunar and Gregorian calendars are different (with the lunar having an extra month every fourth year), Tet does not fall on the same day every year. But the rituals surrounding the festival have been the same for generations.

There is much feasting, not only at home but also when one calls on relatives and friends, with special foods like *banh chung*, or traditional glutinous rice cake. The Vietnamese call it "eating Tet", a celebration which lasts a week but takes longer to prepare. Besides the Tet feast, other frantic preparations include the cleaning of the house, the putting up of decorations and the buying of new clothes.

There are also colourful rituals to perform and taboos to observe, beginning a week earlier, when the first offerings to the kitchen god are made. Thereafter, rituals and taboos are observed from the eve to the seventh day of Tet. These include keeping bad spirits away with gongs and drums, which have replaced the recently banned firecrackers; offering food and incense to ancestors; and avoiding bad and angry thoughts.

The celebration of Tet is a celebration of life. Not merely a formality, it is an occasion when the Vietnamese reaffirm their belief in tradition and family.

Vietnam comes alive on the first day of the first lunar month when the country celebrates Tet. Plum blossoms (top left) are necessary purchases not only for their decorative qualities but as a defence against evil spirits when the normal protectors of the home, the earth and hearth gods, are away in heaven filing reports of their earthly charges' behaviour. Similarly, the din created by firecrackers (far right) and lion dancers (right and above) drive away these spirits, while generous food offerings (top right) appease others.

Before firecrackers were banned in Vietnam, one of its most spectacular celebrations took place in the village of Dong Ky on the fourth day of Tet. The festival was a firecracker competition which saw entries beautifully decorated with symbolic animals in papier-mâché (facing page). So big were these crackers that as many as 24 men were needed to lift them (top left) for the customary parade through the streets (above and right). After village elders and priests (top right) had judged the winner, the crackers were set off to end the festival with a big bang.

Communal Celebrations

The Vietnamese celebrate festivals on three levels—personal, national or communal. National celebrations include Tet and Buddha's birthday. Personal traditions involve only one's family, for example, the death anniversary of an ancestor. Communal celebrations involve the entire village, such as the Dong festival celebrated in Phu Dong village, which simulates the life of a mythical hero.

But the Montagnards, with their many diverse customs, have some of the most unique festivals, all relating to their hope for a good harvest of wildlife or grain. One such festival is the buffalo sacrifice practised by the Tay Nguyen minority. A week before the sacrifice, jars are decorated for the storage of wine and bamboo is selected for the repair of the communal house and the erection of a central totem to which the sacrificial buffalo is tethered.

Before the animal is sacrificed, young men dressed in their ethnic costumes do a war dance accompanied by gongs and drums. Celebrations continue into the night when the meat of the sacrificed animal and jars of wine are served. Dancing and singing accompany the feasting. And as the glow of the campfire is replaced by that of the rising sun, the celebrants return home, happy in the knowledge that they have appeased their god.

Wheel power is highly relied on in Vietnam. No load is too cumbersome as two and three-wheelers are used to transport everything—from dogs to farm produce. Even more amazing is the dexterity with which cyclists manoeuvre overloaded vehicles on typically crowded streets.

VIETNAM VIGNETTES

No one goes to Vietnam without being amazed at the riotous confusion of sights, sounds and smells on its main streets. A farmer balances a huge bundle of vegetables on a bicycle, pedalling among a sea of cyclists. The *cyclo*, the ubiquitous Vietnamese pedicab meant for two, is used to transport a big cabinet and its equally endowed owner. An entire family whooshes by on a Honda cub.

By day, street corners come to life as barbers set up open-air salons and tyre repairers patch up off-mended tubes. At night, hawkers offer steaming bowls of rice noodles. And on Sunday nights, the youngsters of Ho Chi Minh City *chay rong rong*, going round and round the streets along Dong Khoi on hundreds of motorcycles.

Enterprise takes on a new meaning on the streets of Vietnam. One simply strolls down to the street corner for a haircut (top right), which is not complete until the barber gives you a vigorous neck massage and thorough ear cleaning (top left). The guitar seller (above), on the other hand, sets up shop on the quieter back lane while pavements are ideal for shopkeepers selling religious paraphernalia (right) and hardware (far right).

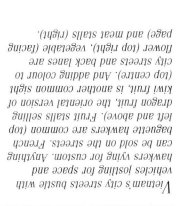

Vietnam's city streets bustle with vehicles jostling for space and hawkers vying for custom. Anything can be sold on the streets. French baguette hawkers are common (top left and above). Fruit stalls selling dragon fruit, the oriental version of kiwi fruit, is another common sight (top centre). And adding colour to city streets and back lanes are flower (top right), vegetable (facing page) and meat stalls (right).

The Reunification Express (this spread) is a misnomer. Although it affords accessibility between Hanoi and Ho Chi Minh City, it takes at least two days to make that journey. It, however, provides city weary tourists escaping from clockwork discipline with an adventurous, if haphazard, ride and locals living around the tracks with a vital source of income.

The Graceful Ao Dai

Schoolgirls cycling home in their white *ao dais* have been likened to floating butterflies. Women in their national dress are described as alluring and provocative. The *ao dai*, the graceful national costume of Vietnamese women, elicits only compliments.

In the mid-18th century, the long skirts worn by Vietnamese women were abandoned for Chinese-inspired coats and trousers. The second Nguyen emperor, Minh Manh, made the wearing of trousers mandatory for the entire female population. It was not until the 1930s that the *ao dai* was modernised, evolving into its present form.

It even suffered a period of disfavour during the austerity drive after the pullout of the American forces. But a woman never forsakes that which enhances her beauty. And so, the *ao dai* continues to charm the world.

*V*ying for space does not stop on city streets (above). Commuters on inter-city buses jostle for space not only with fellow travellers but paraphernalia as well (facing page, bottom right). Hawkers vie not for space but for custom (facing page, bottom left) just as hotels (facing page, top centre and right) compete for guests and dining establishments (facing page, centre and top left) for patrons.

*T*he allure of the ao dai, the Vietnamese woman's national dress, has been explained in many ways. Part mystery, part revelation is one charming description. But no adjective can fully describe the sight of carefree schoolgirls in their white ao dais (top left) or young women in their colourful versions (left).

PART FOUR
ART AND ARCHITECTURE

Had it not been for archaeological relics such as the Dong Son bronze drum, Vietnam's early history would only be told in myths and legends. For unlike other ancient civilisations, the Vietnamese do not have monuments which have withstood the test of time.

Building in wood and materials vulnerable to the tropical weather resulted in the destruction of much of the country's architecture. The little remaining stone structures were decimated in protracted wars. The oldest architectural relic, remnants of the citadel fortress of Co Loa, can be traced to the 3rd century. Nothing earlier than that remains.

So it comes as a surprise that some later pre-modern buildings, despite heavy bombardment during the war with America, did survive. Mainly pagodas, temples, palaces and tombs, they reflect an eclectic mix of Vietnamese tradition with Chinese influence and Buddhist inspiration.

Elaborately carved, colourfully painted and painstakingly decorated with mosaics, many of these historic buildings may have been haphazardly renovated, but they still retain their operatic splendour of yore. For these grand dwellings were raised for the use of gods and kings, sovereigns accustomed to fine art and gracious living. Anything less would be sacrilegious.

What has also survived, though not of Vietnamese origin, are some magnificent Cham towers and sculptures. Relics of the Indianised kingdom of Champa, these splendid Hindu temples boast masonry sophisticated enough to withstand the ravages of both man and nature.

Cham sculpture, like their traditional Vietnamese counterpart, were mainly religious. While Cham sculptors carved sandstone into altars, lingas and images of Shiva, Brahma and Vishnu, early Vietnamese sculptors created statues of deities, heroes and mythical animals from wood and stone. In fact, all early Vietnamese arts, including painting, dance and music, were also rooted in religion.

But Vietnam's artistic legacy extends beyond just the Oriental or the religious. Urban architecture towards the early decades of this century took on a decidedly French accent, owing to a period of French occupation. So did painting, which evolved from traditional renditions of religious and mythological scenes, to calligraphic interpretations of nature with Taoist overtones, before the influence of European renaissance and modern French art set in. What all this means, as one art lover says, is that Vietnamese art has developed a unique combination of Eastern mystery and Western familiarity.

With so much cultural borrowing, one might even be tempted to think that indigenous Vietnamese art and architecture does not exist. After all, a country which has suffered so much devastation would have neither the energy nor resource to pursue more than bread and butter issues. As if existing solely to debunk this misperception is *Roi Nuoc*, the art of water puppetry. Found in no other land, it will convince you, as history and life unfolds on its watery stage, that only a civilisation steeped in culture will have such rich traditions.

The kingdom of Champa enjoyed a short-lived history in Vietnam but left a legacy of brilliant art and architecture, reflected in the elegance of sculptures such as the celestial dancer, Uma (left), and the sophisticated masonry work of brick towers dedicated to Hindu deities (above).

103

CHAM ART—REMNANTS OF AN ANCIENT CIVILISATION

The kingdom of Champa flourished in what is now Southern Vietnam from the 2nd to 15th centuries. By the time the Vietnamese overran the kingdom, the Cham civilisation was already deeply entrenched in Hindu culture. Cham art and architecture, therefore, was very different from that in the rest of Vietnam. Rather, they seem to blend in with the monuments of the neighbouring Khmer state of Cambodia, or even further afield, in Bali.

Magnificent stone towers still stand in My Son and Nha Trang, legacies of this brilliant civilisation. Sandstone carvings of gods, beasts and celestial dancing girls, preserved in the Cham Museum in Danang, still mesmerise with their exquisite beauty and grace. If it had not been for 20th century bombs, much more of these prolific builders' culture would have been preserved.

Their sophisticated masonry speak of an advanced society of skilled craftsmen. While others were building in wood and stone, the Chams constructed with burnt bricks held together by resin from the *cau day* tree. The entire brick structure was then fired with an intense heat for several days, sealing the bricks and resin into a monument which could withstand both time and the elements.

In its heyday, the domain of the Chams stretched from Hue in central Vietnam to Vung Tau in the south. Today, Danang, just south of Hue, has the world's most comprehensive collection of Cham sculptures. Works, such as the bronze Tara (right), are kept in its Museum of Cham Sculpture, and magnificent Cham towers (above) with splendid facades (bottom left and right) are architectural vestiges which attract tourists to the area.

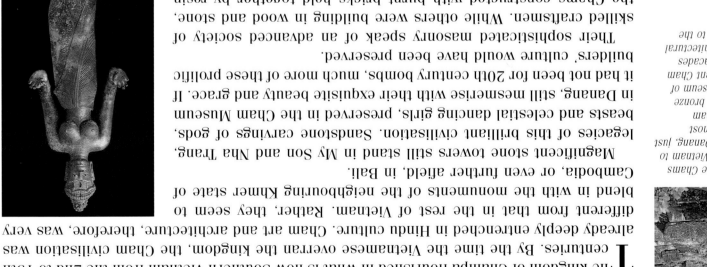

Unlike many Cham relics which exist in isolated patches (right), Po Klong Garai (above) is a complex of four towers built on an arid hill under the reign of the Cham King Jaya Simharvarman III. The descendants of his subjects still live in the surrounding foothills, observing Cham traditions, including worship at the temple complex.

Buddhist influence is strong in Vietnam. A huge statue of Buddha greets devotees in Danang (left) while in Hue, the Thien Mu Pagoda (right) dedicates each level of its seven-storey tower to the worship of one reincarnation of the deity. Although Buddha's image in its various forms and poses (following pages) is worshipped extensively, Vietnamese interpretation allows the worship of other deities (top right).

RELIGIOUS ART AND ARCHITECTURE

Much of Vietnam's architectural vestiges are religious. Borrowing heavily from Chinese Buddhist traditions, these temples were also the springboard of Vietnamese sculpture. The brick and wood constructions housed elaborately carved statues of heroes, gods or mythological animals. Some, like the 11th century Temple of Literature in Hanoi, were more Confucian in spirit while others, like the Thien Mu Pagoda in Hue, were Buddhist in inspiration but Vietnamese in interpretation. Here, Buddha in seven reincarnations is guarded not only by monks and nuns but also by more immortal genies.

The Temple of Literature (above) is clearly Confucian in inspiration while the One Pillar Pagoda (below) can only be described as Chinese in influence. The tiny temple rising from a lotus pond was dedicated to the goddess Kuan Yin by the founder of the Ly Dynasty in gratitude for the deity's bestowal of a male heir.

Despite their Marxist leaning, which is often associated with atheism, the Vietnamese are prolific builders of temples and pagodas. These can range from simple temples (left) to decorative pagodas (right) and elaborate places of worship (below). These religious buildings are, however, bound by a common Chinese and Buddhist inspiration.

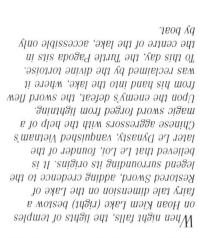

When night falls, the lights of temples on Hoan Kiem Lake (right) bestow a fairy tale dimension on the Lake of Restored Sword, adding credence to the legend surrounding its origins. It is believed that Le Loi, founder of the later Le Dynasty, vanquished Vietnam's Chinese aggressors with the help of a magic sword forged from lightning. Upon the enemy's defeat, the sword flew from his hand into the lake, where it was reclaimed by the divine tortoise. To this day, the Turtle Pagoda sits in the centre of the lake, accessible only by boat.

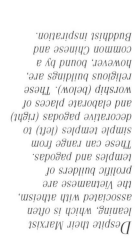

The Holy See

Religious architecture in Vietnam is often classified as Chinese or French in influence. The profusion of Chinese temples and prevalence of Catholic churches bear this out. Sometimes, however, these influences collide, resulting in architectural forms which are considered bizarre to some but quaint to others. One such building is the Holy See at Tay Ninh.

The church towers are European in inspiration; the open sweep of the floor suggests a mosque; and the cobras and dragons adorning the pillars and walls resemble a Buddhist pagoda. From the exterior, it looks like a cross between a Catholic church and a Buddhist temple. But the exotic architecture and paraphernalia speak of an assortment of other influences.

Surprise turns to comprehension when one realises this is the administrative seat of Vietnam's indigenous and colourful religion, Cao Dai. For the religion has something for everyone. Beneath its roof, its followers embrace Christian, Confucian, Buddhist, Islamic and Taoist precepts, revering not only an assortment of gods but mortals such as Winston Churchill and Victor Hugo.

The Vietnamese Dinh

Every Vietnamese village has its *dinh*, or communal house, which serves as a focal point for religious gatherings, village meetings, banquet hall for special occasions and even a village court of sorts.

As it is popularly believed that the fortunes of the villagers depended on the siting of the *dinh*, its building demanded much attention to detail, including religious conformity to geomantic positions. Trees, paths, ponds and yards in and around the *dinh* are carefully arranged so that nature becomes a component of architectural design. Even the interior is not ignored. Master artisans from the land, together with the best workmen from the village, labour at woodcarvings, stone sculpture, colour lacquerwork and gold trimming of altars devoted to the village's guardian spirits.

Architectural influences collide in the Holy See, the temple of the Cao Dai sect (top) while Chinese influence can be detected in the Vietnamese dinh. *Once the focal point of every village, constructed with meticulous attention to detail (far right), the* dinh *is slowly losing its importance and some have been transformed into schools (above) and meeting places (centre).*

The *dinh* may be slowing losing its position of importance as Vietnam turns its attention to more pressing economic issues but its presence stands as a testimony to the existence of a typically Vietnamese structure.

AN ARCHITECTURAL ASSIMILATION

While Vietnam may not have an Angkor like her Khmer neighbour, history has left enough splendid architecture as testimony to the country's ancient traditions. Nowhere is this more obvious than in the temples, pagodas and tombs which can be found all over the land.

Chinese influence is evident in most of these structures, a result of the early and prolonged contact with China. It left such a profound influence that art and architecture in Vietnam closely mirrored that of the Chinese civilisation for many centuries.

French colonisation, which came in the late 19th century, effectively ended this Oriental stranglehold. In fact, French architectural influence was so dominant that the major cities of Hanoi, Ho Chi Minh and Hue still retain enclaves harking back to the Europeans' colonial presence.

The prevalence of these two influences has resulted in an unresolved debate on whether an indigenous Vietnamese architecture exists. It is easy to agree with those who say it does not. Afterall, there is no distinct architectural form as instantly recognisable as that of some civilisations, such as the Thais. But like much else in Vietnam, looking beyond the surface to the details yields a different perspective. The layout plan of most Vietnamese temples, for example, differ from that of the Chinese. And the *dinh*, the communal house found in every village, is planned, built and decorated according to Vietnamese precepts.

While Vietnam's architecture does not astound the senses like Indonesia's Borobudur or stir the soul like India's Taj Mahal, it nevertheless provokes wonder with its fluid combination of other influences. This seamless melding of foreign elements is due largely to the way the Vietnamese have imbibed the cultures of conquering lands, be they Chinese or French, to make them wholly hers.

Built by the Japanese community in the 17th century, the covered Japanese bridge (above and below) once connected the quarters of the Japanese and Chinese merchants living in Hoi An. The wooden Sunbeam Bridge on Hoan Kiem Lake in Hanoi (bottom), on the other hand, was built by locals in the 19th century.

The architecture of the old quarter in Hoi An is a good catalogue of its ancient history. One of the most important trading ports in Southeast Asia for several centuries, it was home to a large community of foreign merchants, including many Japanese and Chinese. The former left behind a legacy of Japanese style shops and houses and the landmark covered bridge, while the latter bequeathed to the coastal town an impressive number of pagodas and clan houses. Many of these have been restored, and though local inhabitants take them for granted (right), they are the reason for tourists flocking to the once flourishing port.

The Imperial City

A millennium of Chinese rule resulted in a strong Chinese influence not only in Vietnamese thinking but in its architectural heritage as well. A wealth of Chinese-inspired relics are found all over Vietnam, but it is in Hue that this influence is showcased on a grand scale.

Here, Vietnam's last royal dynasty, inspired by Beijing's Imperial City, built their version of a fortress-palace complex. Begun by the first of the 13 Nguyen emperors, and continued throughout the reign of the empire by each successive king, 300 palaces, temples, mausoleums, libraries and theatres were built in and around the city's 21-metre thick fortress walls. Seven of these emperors are buried in self-designed mausoleums, complete with pavilions, temples and funeral stelae. Only a third of these monuments survived the war against the French and Americans.

*T*he imperial tombs of seven of Nguyen's 13 kings lie scattered on the hillsides on either side of the Perfume River. All self-designed, they left an architectural heritage which spoke volumes of their designers. The earlier emperors displayed more restraint—from the elegant blending of classical architecture with natural beauty in Minh Manh's tomb (left) to the harmonious majesty of the tombs of Tu Duc (right and below) and Dong Khan (bottom left). However, the penultimate ruler, Khai Dinh, left behind an elaborate cement edifice outstanding for its ostentatious blending of the oriental and occidental (bottom right).

*T*he architecture of Vietnam's Imperial City (facing page) borrowed heavily from its namesake in Beijing, China. It was similarly based on a Confucian political and philosophical conception of the monarch as the centre of the world and the link between heaven and earth.
Enclosed within a moated citadel was the Imperial City (facing page, centre) where the offices of the central government, palaces, libraries, temples and pavilions (facing page, bottom right) were built. The City was accessed via richly decorated gates (facing page, bottom left). Within it was the Forbidden Purple City (facing page, top) the exclusive abode of the immediate imperial family.

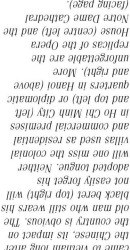

Although French influence came to Vietnam long after the Chinese, its impact on the country is obvious. The old man who still wears his black beret (top right) will not easily forget his adopted tongue. Neither will one miss the colonial villas used as residential and commercial premises in Ho Chi Minh City (left and top left) or diplomatic quarters in Hanoi (above and right). More unforgettable are the replicas of the Opera House (centre left) and the Notre Dame Cathedral (facing page).

French Influence

French influence came to Vietnam long after Chinese culture had been absorbed into the mainstream of Vietnamese life. But with typical Vietnamese alacrity, parts of the country, especially in the major cities, soon took on a distinctly French atmosphere.

Today, many older Vietnamese still speak French and wear black berets. The French baguette is as easily available as any Vietnamese cuisine. But it is in the architecture of enclaves in Hanoi, Ho Chi Minh City and even Hue, the ancient imperial capital, that French influence is most evident.

The baroque-style Opera House in Hanoi may not be as majestic as the original but was built as a replica of its namesake in France. The Art Noveau style of some of the guest houses in Vietnam's capital city, with their wrought-iron fixtures, glass canopies, green shutters and yellow walls are similar to the Metro stations in Paris, while the entire diplomatic quarter, including the US Consulate, is housed in old French villas.

Hue, the showcase of Chinese architectural influence, also has its French quarter of tree-lined boulevards and colonial villas. But the Notre Dame Cathedral shares only the name and elements of the original's Gothic inspiration. Like Cao Dai's Holy See, the cathedral incorporates other influences, in this case modern American and Chinese Buddhist.

The lion's share of French architecture is found in Ho Chi Minh City, which has often been described as a miniature Oriental version of Paris. The city's entertainment and nightlife zone on Dong Khoi Street was once a tree-lined avenue known as the Rue Catinat, popular for its cafes where foreign correspondents gathered. Other landmarks to the colonial era include the earlier but more accurate copy of the Notre Dame Cathedral and the neo-renaissance Hotel de Ville, now occupied as government offices.

TUBE HOUSES

Although found in several other Southeast Asian countries, the tube house is another interesting aspect of architecture which evolved from practical needs. It was a resourceful answer to limited commercial and residential space in the area known as "36 Streets", which has names such as Paper Street and Silver Street, reflecting the trade which congregated on the same lane in times past.

Built in the late 19th or early 20th centuries, tube architecture consisted of long and narrow dwellings, some no more than two metres wide but up to 100 metres long, designed to give each family a room fronting onto the street from which to do business. As cement was not available in Vietnam then, these brick structures were held together with a mixture of sugar-cane juice, sand and lime.

Originally designed to house one family, many of them now hold more than five and sometimes, up to ten, families. Unfortunately, many are falling into disrepair or losing their traditional facades from overzealous renovations.

A CANVAS OF MANY CULTURES

Vietnam's earliest artistic efforts were found in the caves of the Red River Delta. Chinese influence brought calligraphy and silk paintings of nature and landscapes. The French introduced Western Cubist and Impressionistic styles, while communism encouraged the stylised Soviet trend of art with a distinct social message.

Such rich artistic traditions and an early exposure to other cultures would have meant an extremely active art scene. However, it is only now, after lurking in the shadows for years, that Vietnamese artists are enjoying a new-found popularity.

As the country enjoys a growing reputation as the next Asian tourist and business destination, so too has the appeal of her artists to international collectors increased. The years of artistic silence have now given way to an urgent vibrancy. So active is the market that there is a lucrative trade in forgeries.

Some have dismissed this vibrancy as a fad. Others maintain that Vietnamese art appeals because of its unique style resulting from the twin influences of Asian traditions and European colonisation. But whatever the reason for this renaissance, Vietnamese artists have finally gotten the recognition they deserve.

Vietnamese artists are making a splash on the international scene. With growing foreign interest, artists young (far right) and old (above) are picking up their brushes again. Street painters are out in full force (top and facing page) while established ones such as Vuong Mo Thanh (following pages) can now work in their favourite medium without fear of persecution.
With the spotlight turned on artists, Vietnam's poets (following page inset) are receiving less international attention. However, they have always enjoyed a respected position at home as Vietnam is a country with a legacy and love of poetry.

Poetry—Window to the Vietnamese Soul

Vietnam's rich poetic tradition began with oral origins as folk songs, lullabies, work chants and love songs. With Chinese rule came exposure to the great Chinese classics and the flourishing of written prose and poetry. Scholars, monks, kings and court officials were often prolific writers who were held in high esteem by Vietnamese society.

Many of their works are still read and often quoted. Ask any Vietnamese and he'll be able to recite a verse or two from *The Tale of Kieu*, an epic poem of more than 3,000 verses about the love and life of a beautiful courtesan. Kieu's story, which entranced the Vietnamese for 200 years, is steeped in Confucian and Buddhist philosophy.

By the early 20th century, a new generation of poets influenced by Western and French literary forms and philosophies began to create poems exploring personal thoughts and philosophies.

But whatever the inspiration, writing remains a dominant art form in the country, especially since the Vietnamese language, with its six tonal pronunciations for every syllable, is well suited to poetry.

THE PERFORMING ARTS

Music, dance and theatre were inseparable components in pre-modern Vietnam. Village celebrations were incomplete without folk dance and music. With the onset of Chinese influence, an additional form of popular entertainment was introduced. Essentially an adaptation of Chinese opera, Vietnamese theatre became known as *hat boi*, meaning songs with gestures.

Revolutionary music and theatre were introduced along with communism. During the early years, any hint of Western influence in music, dance or theatre was frowned upon. The restrictions have been eased in recent years. Today, pop songs are great favourites among karaoke-singing Vietnamese while youngsters jive to the latest beat in crowded discos.

A Watery Stage

Eight hundred years ago, villagers celebrating the end of the spring rice harvest looked forward with eager anticipation to the spectacular entertainment of battle scenes and dragon dances. The hero was a puppet made of a special light wood resistant to constant exposure to water, often half-a-metre tall and painted in bright colours, whose brave struggle with the enemy on the water was punctuated by firecrackers which spewed smoke and created ripples. Dramatising the action in song were traditional folk opera singers, accompanied by bronze drums, stone gongs and bamboo xylophones.

Today, *Roi Nuoc*, or water puppetry, is still performed with the puppeteer standing in metre-deep waters, manipulating the wooden puppets behind a bamboo curtain with an apparatus hidden in the water. However, the puppeteers don diving suits in winter, instead of relying on *nuoc mam*, or fermented fish sauce, to keep warm.

The origin of this ancient art is unclear but it is believed to have started as a traditional puppet show, which took to the waters when a puppet troop, to avoid disappointing the eager audience, performed in flood waters. The art then spread from its birthplace in the north and is now performed all over Vietnam, having been accorded the status of national treasure by Ho Chi Minh, who founded Hanoi's Water Puppet Theatre.

With the advent of modern music and other leisure pursuits, traditional music, dance and theatre are losing the popularity they once enjoyed. However, as art forms with a long history in Vietnam, they are traditions which will never be left behind. Today, opera (centre right) is performed only in villages and on special occasions. Traditional singers (facing page and centre left), water puppeteers (left, inset) and musicians (top left) are, however, benefiting from the tourist boom.

*T*ourists looking for a typically
Vietnamese souvenir would inevitably
turn to lacquerware. Although it was
introduced from China, the Vietnamese
took to the art with consummate ease,
developing it into a craft which they
are now associated with.
Endless patience is a characteristic
craftsmen must possess as the lacquer
is applied layer by layer (above).
The painstaking labour of these
artisans produce beautiful items such
as boxes (right), doors (top) or statues
(facing page).

A CONSUMMATE CRAFT

I t can be found at every tourist destination. An art which has become synonymous with
Vietnam, lacquerware was introduced into the country from China during the 15th century.
Like much of Vietnam's traditional arts, it was first used in pagodas as ornamental decoration.
But it has since become a thriving industry, providing work for many thousands of skilled
craftsmen and souvenirs for visitors from all over the world. Usually inlaid with ivory or
mother-of-pearl, the art entails meticulous attention to detail. Endless patience is required
as craftsmen painstakingly apply the lacquer layer by layer. Animal, human or landscape
motifs are painted or inlaid during the process, with the finished work taking on a multi-
dimensional effect.

Although the art did not begin here, the Vietnamese contributed extensively to its devel-
opment by expanding its artistic potential with new techniques such as the use of eggshell.
Lacquerware has today become one of the most important art forms in Vietnam.

VIETNAM
THROUGH OLD PHOTOGRAPHS

*H*along Bay was once an important seaport. The lack of mooring facilities, however, forced ships to unload in the middle of the bay, using smaller junks and barges. But traders faced an even greater danger from pirates who hid among the many caves in the bay.

His Majesty Duy Tan, emperor of Annam. Unlike the north and south, known respectively as Tonkin and Cochinchina under French rule, central Vietnam, renamed Annam, was the only region of the country allowed a small degree of self-rule. Although French control was strong, Emperor Duy Tan was allowed to keep his title.

*P*omp and ceremony accompanied the young emperor Duy Tan, the chosen Son of Heaven, wherever he went. Official outings were grand affairs involving an entourage of sedan bearers, armed escorts and attendants.

*T*he mandarins (top left), as officials in the emperor's court, enjoyed privileges not extended to the common man. Like the emperor, he travelled with armed escorts (top right), although his entourage was much smaller (bottom right). He also did not have at his beck and call, royal transport including elephants, usually used on hunting trips (bottom left).

*E*laborately embroidered imperial finery was worn only by royalty and the mandarins, with the royal dragon featured prominently. Court etiquette and finery were all modelled closely on that of the Chinese.

One Pillar Pagoda, built in the 11th century by the founder of the Lý Dynasty in honour of the goddess Kuan Yin, was destroyed during the last years of French rule. Photographic records and its petite structure allowed a reconstruction of the original.

*E*mperor Gia Long embarked on a massive construction of the Nguyen Dynasty's capital in Hue when he came into power. Eighty thousand men were drafted to build a French-style Citadel around a Chinese-inspired Imperial City. The best artisans worked on decorative details such as these huge bronze urns on the grounds of the City.

*T*he rich made offerings at elaborate altars, such as this, for answered prayers (left). When the answered prayer also involved a fiscal windfall, an opera troupe (such as the one above) may be invited to perform. The only entertainment available in villages, opera performances—held at the village đình or the home of the opera patron—were eagerly awaited.

Women from the minority Meo tribe still wear the same traditional costumes as their ancestors (left). The northern delta lady (above), however, has changed her attire into the more alluring ao dai.

Before the advent of the ao dai, the design of traditional dress distinguished the social class of the wearer. Landed gentry wore long coats and trousers in brocade and silk (top left and right) while peasants wore loose tunics and trousers in cotton (bottom left). Tribesmen dressed in their own style, much the same way as they do now (bottom right).

A village in northern Vietnam's Cao Bang in the 19th century (top). The cyclos we see on Vietnam's streets now probably evolved from the one-wheeled cart, the only man-made transport for hire in rural villages in those days (bottom).

Hanoi's European quarters on Rue Paul Bert boasted wide boulevards and European architecture adapted to the tropics. Façades, decorated with carved pillars and gables, added to the grandeur of the buildings. All these houses could not, however, rival the opulence of the Opera House at the end of the street.

*N*ative quarters on *Rue Des Changeurs*, on the other hand, featured a narrow street lined by Chinese inspired houses. The facades, except for the Chinese temple in the foreground, were less fussy than that of their European counterpart.

A panoramic view of Hanoi's European quarters reveals a distinct European layout with wide tree-lined boulevards and sparse arrangement of accommodations.